THE
DESIGN
OF
ECONOMIC
ACCOUNTS

Nancy Ruggles

and Richard Ruggles, *Yale University*

NATIONAL BUREAU OF ECONOMIC RESEARCH

NEW YORK   1970

DISTRIBUTED BY COLUMBIA UNIVERSITY PRESS

NEW YORK AND LONDON

RELATION OF THE DIRECTORS
TO THE WORK AND PUBLICATIONS
OF THE NATIONAL BUREAU OF ECONOMIC RESEARCH

1. The object of the National Bureau of Economic Research is to ascertain and to present to the public important economic facts and their interpretation in a scientific and impartial manner. The Board of Directors is charged with the responsibility of ensuring that the work of the National Bureau is carried on in strict conformity with this object.

2. The President of the National Bureau shall submit to the Board of Directors, or to its Executive Committee, for their formal adoption all specific proposals for research to be instituted.

3. No research report shall be published until the President shall have submitted to each member of the Board the manuscript proposed for publication, and such information as will, in his opinion and in the opinion of the author, serve to determine the suitability of the report for publication in accordance with the principles of the National Bureau. Each manuscript shall contain a summary drawing attention to the nature and treatment of the problem studied, the character of the data and their utilization in the report, and the main conclusions reached.

4. For each manuscript so submitted, a special committee of the Board shall be appointed by majority agreement of the President and Vice Presidents (or by the Executive Committee in case of inability to decide on the part of the President and Vice Presidents), consisting of three directors selected as nearly as may be one from each general division of the Board. The names of the special manuscript committee shall be stated to each Director when the manuscript is submitted to him. It shall be the duty of each member of the special manuscript committee to read the manuscript. If each member of the manuscript committee signifies his approval within thirty days of the transmittal of the manuscript, the report may be published. If at the end of that period any member of the manuscript committee withholds his approval, the President shall then notify each member of the Board, requesting approval or disapproval of publication, and thirty days additional shall be granted for this purpose. The manuscript shall then not be published unless at least a majority of the entire Board who shall have voted on the proposal within the time fixed for the receipt of votes shall have approved.

5. No manuscript may be published, though approved by each member of the special manuscript committee, until forty-five days have elapsed from the transmittal of the report in manuscript form. The interval is allowed for the receipt of any memorandum of dissent or reservation, together with a brief statement of his reasons, that any member may wish to express; and such memorandum of dissent or reservation shall be published with the manuscript if he so desires. Publication does not, however, imply that each member of the Board has read the manuscript, or that either members of the Board in general or the special committee have passed on its validity in every detail.

6. Publications of the National Bureau issued for informational purposes concerning the work of the Bureau and its staff, or issued to inform the public of activities of Bureau staff, and volumes issued as a result of various conferences involving the National Bureau shall contain a specific disclaimer noting that such publication has not passed through the normal review procedures required in this resolution. The Executive Committee of the Board is charged with review of all such publications from time to time to ensure that they do not take on the character of formal research reports of the National Bureau, requiring formal Board approval.

7. Unless otherwise determined by the Board or exempted by the terms of paragraph 6, a copy of this resolution shall be printed in each National Bureau publication.

(Resolution adopted October 25, 1926, and revised February 6, 1933,
February 24, 1941, and April 20, 1968)

CONTENTS

TABLES

FIGURES

PREFACE

National income accounting has evolved from the combined efforts of economists in universities, research organizations, national governments, and international organizations. The results of these efforts have been discussed at the conferences of the International Association for Research in Income and Wealth and the Conference on Income and Wealth sponsored by the National Bureau of Economic Research. This present study synthesizes many of the ideas presented at these conferences. In addition, the system of national accounts developed for the Yale Economic Growth Center as a framework for their studies of less developed countries has provided a testing ground for a number of the ideas presented.

The immediate impetus for this study was the proposed revision of the United Nations System of National Accounts, which has stimulated discussion of this topic. It is clear that the present form of national economic accounting should be revised; the purpose of this study is to examine both the present United States system and the proposed United Nations system in the light of specific needs for new concepts, new types of information, and the potentiality of data processing provided by the newer computer technologies.

We are especially indebted to George Jaszi of the Office of Business Economics of the U. S. Department of Commerce and his staff; in particular, Irving Rottenberg, Chief of the National Income Division, saved us from making a number of serious errors and John Gorman was very helpful with the treatment of financial transactions. We owe a great deal to John Kendrick and his work at the National Bureau of Economic Research on the conceptual changes and the broad economic constructs.

In a number of cases, we have relied heavily on both his concepts and his estimates, which are not yet published.

Many people at the National Bureau of Economic Research have contributed to this work. Two staff reading committees, consisting of John Kendrick, Richard Easterlin, Victor Fuchs, David Kresge, and Peter Temin, reviewed earlier drafts of the manuscript and made helpful suggestions. Boris Shishkin, Robert A. Charpie, and Thomas D. Flynn, members of the Board of Directors' Reading Committee, were particularly helpful in their comments. We also thank Virginia Meltzer, who edited the manuscript.

1 INTRODUCTION

The Objectives of National Economic Accounting

National economic accounting has as its prime objective the creation of an information framework suitable for analyzing the operation of the economic system. A modern economic system operates on the basis of a network of transactions. Individuals receive compensation for their labor or for their ownership of assets, and they use this compensation for purchasing consumption needs or for acquiring assets. Business firms buy goods and services from other business firms, and pay for labor or other factor services that they use. In turn they sell their output on the market. Governments collect taxes from individuals and business, and provide a wide range of public services and transfer payments. Assets are bought and sold, and liabilities are incurred and paid off. In fact, a bewildering mass of transactions takes place simultaneously. In analyzing the operation of the economy or in evaluating its performance the economist must consider information on this flow of transactions as a major part of his basic data.

Although market transactions provide the basis of national economic accounting, all market transactions need not be recorded in the accounts. In some cases it is only necessary to use the net change resulting from a group of transactions: thus, in observing the stock of goods held, interest may focus on the net change from period to period, rather than on the total flowing into the stock and the total flowing out. Many other transactions are trivial, and add little to an explanation of the operation of the economy. Relatively unimportant agency functions may be consolidated out: for example, an individual's action in changing the denomination of his currency so that he can carry out smaller transactions can be ignored. Most transactions have economic meaning, however, and the national economic accounting framework should provide a systematic and comprehensive treatment of these transactions so that the operation of the system is portrayed accurately.

To provide a complete picture of economic activity, it is often necessary to impute transactions in situations where important economic activity is taking place but no market transaction occurs. Internal bookkeeping represents one major class of such imputed transactions. Such factors as depreciation of capital and changes in equity should be reflected in the accounts even though these bookkeeping entries involve no actual market transactions. Another type of imputed transaction records nonmarket economic activity taking place within economic units. In many countries the amount of such nonmarket economic activity is considerable: farmers produce food for their own use; and individuals owning their own homes receive a flow of services from home ownership. Finally, imputed transactions are required where payment or trade between economic units takes place in kind. Employees, for example, may receive food and shelter as part of their compensation, or a depositor may receive banking services in exchange for the use of his deposits. Also, in some countries barter of goods and services may occur on a significant scale.

The transactions data must be organized and presented so that the behavior and interaction of the major parts of the system will be revealed and the structural changes taking place in the system can be understood. Because the economic system is in general equilibrium, different macroeconomic problems will be directly related to one another, and the national economic accounting framework can serve as an integrating device. To be useful in economic models that are intended to analyze the interactions among different parts of the economic system, the national accounts must provide suitable methods of disaggregation and deconsolidation so that these interrelationships can be observed and measured.

Although a system of classification or arrangement may imply an economic model, it does not follow that a specific economic model should underlie the design of a national economic accounting system. A number of different models may have similar information requirements. The adequacy of a given national economic accounting framework should be judged by (1) whether it can provide the basic information required for the major classes of economic models, and (2) whether it can avoid presenting information not required for any reasonable economic model.

Such a system must be able to meet the information requirements of a wide variety of uses. It has long been recognized that national accounts information is required for studies of income determination, and it is becoming increasingly clear that studies of production functions, balance of payments, monetary policy, capital formation, income distribution, and similar problems must all be carried out in terms of their setting in the economic system as a whole. For these uses, accounts must provide both the general framework within which the interaction takes place and the detailed economic information needed for specific analysis of the different problems.

The Elements of National Economic Accounts

For evaluating its design, an economic accounting system can be considered to possess certain characteristics. These are (1) the structure of the national income accounts in terms of the types of economic activities and the sectoring of transactors in the economy, (2) the economic constructs on which these accounts are based, and (3) the method of integration of the national income accounts with other national economic accounts and related data.

The Structure

The concept of an account is basic to the development of a national income accounting system. Accounts provide the framework for recording actual or imputed sets of transactions. An account may be drawn up for any specific type of economic activity that the economist finds useful. Thus, the economist desiring to record current economic activity may focus on production, consumption, capital formation, redistribution of income, or any other block of transactions he wishes to use. The literature of national accounting abounds with different kinds of accounts drawn up for a variety of purposes. For a national income accounting system, the accounts chosen must provide systematic coverage of all economic activity, and unnecessary detail and redundancy must be avoided.

The structure of the system, however, also depends on the sectors of the economy. Customarily, sectors refer to particular groups of transactors. Thus, for example, accounts may be set up for sectors composed of particular industries, business firms, households, governments, nonprofit institutions, etc. It is by the use of sectors that the economist can delineate the transactions network among various groups in the economic system. In the last analysis, it is sometimes hard to distinguish between a type of economic activity and sectoring of the economy. For example, considerable difficulty arises in the case of international transactions: many national income accounting systems consider the set of external transactions to be a particular type of economic activity, whereas other systems arrive at similar results by setting up a foreign or rest of the world sector. In spite of these difficulties, however, it is useful to consider the structure of a national income accounting system in terms of a two-fold classification consisting of (a) the type of economic activity for which transactions are classified and (b) the division of the economy into sectors of transactors.

The Economic Constructs of National Income Accounts

The concept of national income was originally intended to measure the economic welfare of the system in terms of the income produced. With the further development of macroeconomic theory, additional economic constructs such as gross national product, consumption expenditures, capital formation, personal income, and disposable income were introduced; as national income accounting has developed, these and other economic constructs have provided much of the content of the system. To an increasing extent, however, economists working on more elaborate economic models have found a need for further disaggregation and deconsolidation of the major economic constructs into their component parts.

The economic constructs contained in the accounts must provide identifiable economic variables which are important for economic analysis. The success of economic research depends upon the development of operational concepts capable of statistical measurement. Without analytically useful constructs, the content of the national income accounts becomes meaningless. Instead of providing the analyst with a coherent body of useful information, it will merely contain a confusing mass of detail.

The Integration of National Income Accounts With Other Economic Accounts and Related Data

Although most of this discussion has been in terms of national income accounts, these are not the only forms of national economic accounts. Almost all countries now have some form of national income accounts, many have input-output tables, some have sets of financial accounts, and a small but increasing number have wealth accounts or balance sheets. The degree of integration among these accounts differs widely from country to country, as does the degree to which these economic accounts are integrated with the large body of other social and economic information. In very few, if any, countries are all of these forms of economic accounting systematically related to one another.

The integration of national income accounts with other economic accounts and with the related economic and social data is important for the future development of economic information systems. Many of our recent economic models require a wide variety of information. For example, models designed to measure the effect of government fiscal and monetary policy not only require the information contained in the national income accounts to appraise the impact of a change in the tax structure upon individuals and businesses, but they also require financial data to evaluate the repercussions in areas like housing, consumer credit, and business investment. These repercussions in turn must be examined in the context of output, productivity, and employment in such industries as construction, automobiles, and producers durables. Recent interest in the problems of poverty, similarly, has emphasized the need for investigating selective effects of changes in the level of economic activity and prices on such socioeconomic groups as the unskilled and less educated or the fixed income retired population.

In this context, a national economic accounting system should provide the general framework into which all economic and social data can be fitted. This does not mean that it is the duty of the national accountant to specify all of the social information needed for all social problems. It does mean that it is very important for the economic accounting system to provide for the integration of social and economic data so that the direct and indirect effects of the operation of the economic system on social factors can be examined. Conversely, it should be possible to evaluate the effects of both programmed and unprogrammed social changes on the economic system.

Evaluating the Design of National Economic Accounts

Almost all countries have distinctive national accounting systems, with some similarities but also wide differences in basic concepts and in the treatment of specific problems. In addition, a considerable number of ideal or standardized systems have been proposed. A systematic coverage of all of these actual and proposed systems would be a considerable task—one that would discourage even the most avid national accountant. A more manageable approach is to confine the analysis to the national economic accounting systems of the United States and the United Nations. The last major revision of the United States system occurred approximately a decade ago and the current United Nations System of National Accounts is even older. The United Nations has recently revised its system. The revisions were reviewed by the International Association for Research in Income and Wealth in 1965 and the Conference on Income and Wealth in 1966. Both of these conferences raised a number of issues that seemed to warrant further exploration.

The new UN revision represents a significant departure from the present US system. It suggests a radical change in the form and quantity of information in order to integrate a number of different forms of economic accounting into a single system, and it gives somewhat less attention to the major intersectoral relationships and the economic rationale underlying the major economic constructs. In considering the design of a new economic accounting system, therefore, it is useful to evaluate the US and UN systems in terms of the design characteristics of national economic accounting set forth above, and to suggest alternatives to them. The evaluation of the various systems and the economic rationale of possible alternatives will be discussed in Chapters 2, 3, 4, and 5, and in Chapters 6 and 7 the alternatives will be presented in the form of proposed national economic accounts.

Chapter 2 examines the structure of the US and UN systems of national income accounts in terms of the types of economic accounts and the major sectoring of transactors employed, and makes specific recommendations. Chapter 3 evaluates the major economic constructs in these accounts and considers the implications of possible alternatives for the measurement of specific economic constructs. Chapter 4 discusses the integration of the national income accounts with other economic accounts and with related data, giving special consideration to the questions of the role of a data framework and how data should be provided to the analyst. Chapter 5 examines the classification systems and their relation to the integration of economic accounts. Chapter 6 sets forth a proposal for a national income accounting system embodying many of the suggestions relating to types of accounts, sectoring, and economic constructs made in Chapters 2 and 3. The estimates presented in this chapter and in Appendix C will provide the reader with some idea of the nature and magnitude of the proposed revisions, but the estimates are not intended to serve as basic statistical information. Chapter 7 and Appendix C present a proposal for the integration of the other economic accounts and related data with the national income accounts. These sections are in outline form only. Although data are available to implement many parts of the proposed system, a full implementation is beyond the resources of this study. It is reasonable to believe, of course, that the process of implementation would suggest some modifications in the content of the system.

2 THE STRUCTURE OF NATIONAL INCOME ACCOUNTING

The Background of the United States System

National income accounting in the United States is in large measure the result of an evolutionary process initiated by early studies of national income measurement. In 1920 the National Bureau of Economic Research produced as its first publication a study entitled *Income in the United States,* by W. C. Mitchell, W. I. King, F. R. Macaulay, and O. W. Knauth [4]. During the twenties the Bureau published three additional volumes on national income and the incomes of individual states, written by Knauth, Leven, and King [5, 6, 7]. The Bureau's research of this period culminated in the basic study by Willford King, published in 1930 [8].

The depression of the thirties with its precipitous decline in income and employment emphasized the need for more comprehensive information on national income. Concepts were developed and sharpened in this period. The classic works written by Simon Kuznets in this field, dating from the late thirties, provided the basis for future development [9]. Largely because of the Bureau's interest, the Conference on Research in Income and Wealth was established, and in the years since 1937 it has published over 30 volumes on this topic. In the late thirties, the Department of Commerce established a National Income Division, which had the responsibility for preparing current estimates of national income data on an official basis.

The thirties also saw the major development of economic theory that was to convert the field of national income measurement into national income accounting. The Keynesian formulation of income as the sum of consumption and investment focused attention on the final-use breakdown of output, and emphasized the equality of savings and the accumulation of goods. The Keynesian theory also focused attention on the relationship between consumers and producers, and thus fostered the development of sector accounts that articulated the intersectoral network of income and expenditure transactions.

With the outbreak of World War II, it became obvious that considerably more comprehensive statistical information was needed on the operation of the economic system in order to answer such questions as how large a rearmament program or war effort the economic system could support, and how much inflation would be generated by putting the economy on a war footing. The existing statistics on national income and its various breakdowns were not adequate for such analysis, and the National Income Division under Milton Gilbert and George Jaszi enlarged the framework of the statistical system and developed output and income estimates based on the more comprehensive concept of gross national product [10]. During the war, the national income framework and the data were steadily improved. New economic constructs, such as gross capital formation, government expenditures on goods and services, personal income, and disposable income, came into being. Although during this period the data were not published in an accounting form, the framework for the transactions data was explicitly based on the receipts and outlays of government, business, and individuals.

In 1947, the National Income Division cast its published data into an accounting form for the first time [11]. Six accounts were presented, including a national income and product account showing both the gross national product and the national income; sector accounts for business, government, households, and the rest of the world; and a savings and investment account for the economy as a whole. These accounts had as one of their major purposes the derivation of the gross product originating in each of the sectors; less accent was placed on creating a system of intersectoral flows intended as the basis for analysis. A set of 48 supporting tables built around the accounts provided the national income accounting statistics for the period 1929–46, together with related supplementary data at detailed levels of classification. National income and the various types of income payments were shown by industry, as was employment. Detailed data were provided on personal consumption expenditures by type, and special tables reconciled the national income accounts with the savings estimates of the Securities and Exchange Commission and the corporate profits data of the Bureau of Internal Revenue. Additional data were provided on special flows such as new construction activity, producer durable equipment, transfer payments, and interest. Quarterly data were shown for some of the breakdowns in the different accounts, and monthly data were given for personal income by type of income. Thus, by 1947 the national income accounts had emerged for the United States as the basic set of information on the operation of the economic system.

During the next decade there was substantial improvement in the quality of the statistical data and the kind of detailed information provided. In 1954, the National Income Division under George Jaszi published a National Income Supplement [12], which provided extensive information on the sources and methods used in constructing national income, and presented statistical data on a comparable revised basis for the period from 1929 to 1953.

Additional work on national economic accounting was done by other parts of the government in this period. The work on input-output initiated in 1939 by Wassily Leontief [13] was carried on by the Bureau of Labor Statistics, and resulted in an input-output table for the year 1947 [14]. The pioneering work of Morris Copeland on moneyflows [15] was taken over by the Federal Reserve Board and data on the flow of funds were published for the period from 1939 on [16].

To consider the interrelationships of these different forms of national economic accounting, a National Accounts Review Committee under the direction of the National Bureau of Economic Research was appointed by the Bureau of the Budget in 1956. This committee surveyed all the existing forms of economic accounting, and made recommendations for a closer integration of the different forms. Relatively few recommendations were made concerning the major economic constructs in the national income accounts, and relatively minor changes in the accounts themselves were suggested [17].

The Office of Business Economics had during this period been preparing a revision of the national income accounts, and in 1958 brought out a version with a somewhat simpler accounting structure and an increased body of data.[1] In this period the OBE also undertook the task of preparing input-output tables, and later published one for the year 1958 on a basis that is statistically integrated with the national

---

[1] See in particular [1], pp. 118–231.

income accounts. The national income accounting system developed in 1958 is still in current use in the United States, but the primarily statistical revision published in 1966 [18] has provided additional detail and increased accuracy.

The Present United States System

The present US national income accounting system consists of five interlocking accounts: National Income and Product Account, Personal Income and Outlay Account, Government Receipts and Expenditures Account, Foreign Transactions Account, and Gross Saving and Investment Account. These accounts are shown in summary form for the year 1966 in Table 1.

The National Income and Product Account provides a consolidated production account for the economy as a whole. The right-hand side of the account shows the output of the nation in terms of the expenditure of the different sectors for consumption and capital formation, together with imports and exports. The left-hand side of the account shows the income payments, taxes, and retained earnings that are generated by the productive activity of the economy. The Personal Income and Outlay Account shows on the right-hand side the income received by households and nonprofit institutions serving households, and on the left-hand side the taxes, outlays, and saving of the sector. The Government Receipts and Expenditures Account shows government receipts in terms of types of taxes on the right-hand side, and on the left-hand side, government expenditures in terms of purchases of goods and services, transfer payments, net interest, subsidies, and the surplus or deficit of the government. The Foreign Transactions Account shows imports of goods and services, net transfer payments, and net foreign investment on the right-hand side, and exports of goods and services on the left-hand side. The Gross Saving and Investment Account collects on the right-hand side all of the savings elements in the system, and balances them with the gross private domestic investment and net foreign investment. Four different types of account are thus shown: (1) a production account for the economy as a whole, (2) income and outlay accounts for the household and nonprofit institution sector and for the general government sector, (3) an external transactions account, and (4) a saving and investment account on a consolidated basis for all sectors of the economy.

TABLE 1

The US System: Summary National Income and Product Accounts, 1966

(billions of dollars)

1. National Income and Product Account

Line				Line			
1	Compensation of employees		435.7	24	Personal consumption expenditures (2–3)		465.9
2	Wages and salaries		394.6	25	Durable goods		70.3
3	Disbursements (2–7)		394.6	26	Nondurable goods		207.5
4	Wage accruals less disbursements (5–4)		.0	27	Services		188.1
5	Supplements to wages and salaries		41.1	28	Gross private domestic investment (5–1)		118.0
6	Employer contributions for social insurance (3–14)		20.3	29	Fixed investment		104.6
				30	Nonresidential		80.2
7	Other labor income (2–8)		20.8	31	Structures		27.9
8	Proprietors' income (2–9)		59.3	32	Producer durable equipment		52.3
9	Rental income of persons (2–10)		19.4	33	Residential structures		24.4
				34	Change in business inventories		13.4
10	Corporate profits and inventory valuation adjustment		82.2	35	Net exports of goods and services		5.1
11	Profits before tax		83.8	36	Exports (4–1)		43.0
12	Profits tax liability (3–11)		34.5	37	Imports (4–2)		37.9
13	Profits after tax		49.3	38	Government purchases of goods and services (3–1		154.3
14	Dividends (2–11)		21.5	39	Federal		77.0
15	Undistributed profits (5–5)		27.8	40	National defense		60.5
16	Inventory valuation adjustment (5–6)		−1.6	41	Other		16.5
17	Net interest (2–13)		20.2	42	State and local		77.2
18	NATIONAL INCOME		616.7				
19	Business transfer payments (2–17)		2.7				
20	Indirect business tax and nontax liability (3–12)		65.1				
21	*Less:* Subsidies less current surplus of government enterprises (3–6)		2.2				
22	Capital consumption allowances (5–7)		63.5				
23	Statistical discrepancy (5–9)		−2.6				

CHARGES AGAINST GROSS
NATIONAL PRODUCT   743.3

GROSS NATIONAL
PRODUCT   743.3

(continued)

TABLE 1 (continued)
2. Personal Income and Outlay Account

Line			Line		
1	Personal tax and nontax payments (3–10)	75.2	7	Wage and salary disbursements (1–3)	394.6
2	Personal outlays	479.0	8	Other labor income (1–7)	20.8
3	Personal consumption expenditures (1–24)	465.9	9	Proprietors' income (1–8)	59.3
4	Interest paid by consumers (2–15)	12.4	10	Rental income of persons (1–9)	19.4
5	Personal transfer payments to foreigners, net (4–4)	.6	11	Dividends (1–14)	21.5
			12	Personal interest income	42.4
6	Personal saving (5–3)	29.8	13	Net interest (1–17)	20.2
			14	Net interest paid by government (3–5)	9.9
			15	Interest paid by consumers (2–4)	12.4
			16	Transfer payments to persons	43.9
			17	From business (1–19)	2.7
			18	From government (3–3)	41.2
			19	*Less:* Personal contributions for social insurance (3–15)	17.9
	PERSONAL TAXES, OUTLAYS, AND SAVING	**584.0**		**PERSONAL INCOME**	**584.0**

3. Government Receipts and Expenditures Account

1	Purchases of goods and services (1–38)	154.3	10	Personal tax and nontax payments (2–1)	75.2
2	Transfer payments	43.5	11	Corporate profits tax liability (1–12)	34.5
3	To persons (2–18)	41.2			
4	To foreigners, net (4–3)	2.3	12	Indirect business tax and nontax liability (1–20)	65.1
5	Net interest paid (2–14)	9.9	13	Contributions for social insurance	38.2
6	Subsidies less current surplus of government enterprises (1–21)	2.2	14	Employer (1–6)	20.3
			15	Personal (2–19)	17.9
7	Surplus or deficit (−), national income and product accounts (5–8)	3.2			
8	Federal	.3			
9	State and local	2.9			
	GOVERNMENT EXPENDITURES AND SURPLUS	**213.0**		**GOVERNMENT RECEIPTS**	**213.0**

(continued)

TABLE 1 (concluded)

4. Foreign Transactions Account

Line			Line		
1	Exports of goods and services (1–36)	43.0	2	Imports of goods and services (1–37)	37.9
			3	Transfer payments from US government to foreigners, net (3–4)	2.3
			4	Personal transfer payments to foreigners, net (2–5)	.6
			5	Net foreign investment (5–2)	2.2
RECEIPTS FROM FOREIGNERS		43.0	**PAYMENTS TO FOREIGNERS**		43.0

5. Gross Saving and Investment Account

Line			Line		
1	Gross private domestic investment (1–28)	118.0	3	Personal saving (2–6)	29.8
2	Net foreign investment (4–5)	2.2	4	Wage accruals less disbursements (1–4)	.0
			5	Undistributed corporate profits (1–15)	27.8
			6	Corporate inventory valuation adjustment (1–16)	−1.6
			7	Capital consumption allowances (1–22)	63.5
			8	Government surplus or deficit (−), national income and product accounts (3–7)	3.2
			9	Statistical discrepancy (1–23)	−2.6
GROSS INVESTMENT		120.2	**GROSS SAVING AND STATISTICAL DISCREPANCY**		120.2

SOURCE: *Survey of Current Business,* July 1967.

NOTE: Numbers in parentheses indicate accounts and items of counter-entry in the accounts.

Two sectors of the economy are shown explicitly: the household and nonprofit institution sector and the general government sector. Households and nonprofit institutions are combined for two reasons: nonprofit institutions do provide consumption of a private nature, and nonprofit institutions, unlike other business enterprises, are not motivated by considerations of profit. Nonprofit institutions included in the household sector are confined to those which furnish services to individuals. This includes religious organizations, social and athletic clubs, labor organizations, nonprofit schools and hospitals, and charitable and welfare organizations. Nonprofit organizations such as mutual savings banks, cooperatives, and other activities primarily of an enterprise nature are excluded from the household and nonprofit institution sector. The nonprofit institutions that are included in the household sector do engage in productive activity, private consumption, and capital formation. Production can also originate in households proper in the US accounts; specifically, households can employ domestic servants. The services of owner-occupied houses, however, are included in the enterprise sector, and households proper have no fixed capital formation.

The general government sector in the US accounts covers all of those activities of the federal, state, and local governments that are not of an enterprise nature. The general government engages in productive activity by hiring government employees. In the US accounts, the government does not engage in fixed capital formation. Expenditures on construction and equipment that in the enterprise sector would be considered fixed capital formation are considered current outlays when made by the general government.

Although there is no explicit enterprise sector in the US accounts, those productive activities that are not specifically included in the household and nonprofit institution sector or in the general government sector can be considered to be enterprise activities. In the 1947 system there was both a business sector and a rest of the world sector. In the present US system, these two groups together constitute the enterprise sector. The rest of the world is included in the enterprise sector because the consolidated production account for the economy shows national rather than domestic productive activity and the payments of national rather than domestic income. Had the consolidated production account for the economy been drawn up to show domestic income and product and domestic income payments, the enterprise sector would by definition have excluded rest of the world activities and there would need to be a separate rest of the world sector. The National Income and Product Account also serves the function of an income and .outlay account for enterprises, showing how the income of enterprises is distributed among employees, owners of capital, and payment of taxes to the government, or retained within the corporate sector.

The structure of the US accounts is shown in Figure 1. The rows in this figure indicate the three sectors of the economy: enterprises, households and nonprofit institutions, and the general government. The columns show the four types of accounts used to record economic activity: production, income and outlay, external transactions, and capital formation. The five accounts of the US national income accounts are entered in the diagram as boxes that indicate the sector and activity coverage of each account. The National Income and Product Account is shown as a consolidated production account for all sectors, and, in addition as an income and outlay account for the enterprise sector. The Personal Income and Outlay Account and the Government Receipts and Expenditures Account are shown as separate income and outlay accounts for the household and nonprofit institution sector and the general government sector. The Foreign Transactions Account is shown as a consolidated account for external transactions. The Gross Saving and Investment Account is consolidated for enterprises and nonprofit institutions but, since in the US accounts the general government does not engage in capital formation, the consolidation does not include this sector.

The Old United Nations System

The old United Nations System of National Accounts [2] was adopted in 1952. In large measure it reflected the development of the national income accounting framework in a number of countries during World War II. Although the work in the United Kingdom and the United States is best known, substantial work on national income accounts was also done in Norway and the Netherlands. In 1940 Ragnar Frisch published a study entitled *National Accounting* [19], and in 1941 the Central Bureau of Statistics of the Netherlands developed a system based on the national bookkeeping concepts of Ed. van Kleef [20]. In 1946 Richard Stone prepared for the League of Nations a monograph on social accounting that was to become the cornerstone for the further development of the field [21]. Many of the European countries under-

FIGURE 1

The Structure of the US System of National Income Accounts

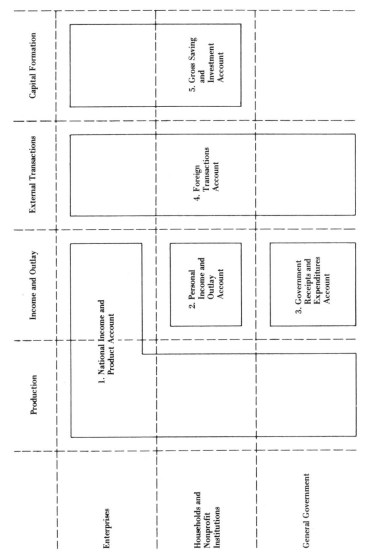

took the compilation of national accounts at this time in order to help in planning economic recovery, and the Organisation for European Economic Cooperation fostered this development by using national income accounting as a basis for its planning. The OEEC set up a National Accounts Research Unit under Richard Stone in Cambridge, England, which developed a standardized system of national accounts for the use of the OEEC; this system with some modification later became the "System of National Accounts" adopted by the United Nations, and shown in Table 2.

TABLE 2

The Old UN System of National Accounts and Supporting Tables:
The Standard Accounts

Account 1. Domestic Product

1.1 Net domestic product at factor cost (2.9)	1.5 Private consumption expenditure (4.1)
1.2 Provisions for domestic fixed capital consumption (3.4 + 4.14 + 5.17)	1.6 General government consumption expenditure (5.1)
1.3 Indirect taxes (5.8)	1.7 Gross domestic fixed capital formation (3.1)
1.4 *Less* subsidies −(5.2)	1.8 Increase in stocks (3.2)
	1.9 Exports of goods and services (6.1)
	1.10 *Less* imports of goods and services −(6.4)
GROSS DOMESTIC PRODUCT AT MARKET PRICES	EXPENDITURE ON GROSS DOMESTIC PRODUCT

Account 2. National Income

2.1 Compensation of employees (4.7)	2.9 Net domestic product at factor cost (1.1)
2.2 Income from unincorporated enterprises (4.8)	2.10 Net factor income from the rest of the world (6.2)
2.3 Income from property (4.9)	
2.4 Saving of corporations (3.3)	
2.5 Direct taxes on corporations (5.9)	
2.6 General government income from property and entrepreneurship (5.6)	
2.7 *Less* interest on the public debt (5.7)	
2.8 *Less* interest on consumers' debt −(4.2)	
NATIONAL INCOME	NET NATIONAL PRODUCT AT FACTOR COST

(continued)

TABLE 2 (continued)

Account 3. Domestic Capital Formation

3.1	Gross domestic fixed capital formation (1.7)	3.3	Saving of corporations (2.4)
3.2	Increase in stocks (1.8)	3.4	Provisions for fixed capital consumption in corporations (1.2*)
		3.5	Net capital transfers to corporations (5.14 + 6.8 − 4.15)
		3.6	Net borrowing of corporations −(4.18 + 5.19 + 6.11)
			Finance of gross capital formation in corporations
		3.7	Finance of gross capital formation in noncorporate private sector (4.12)
		3.8	Finance of gross capital formation in noncorporate public sector (5.13)
GROSS DOMESTIC CAPITAL FORMATION		FINANCE OF GROSS DOMESTIC CAPITAL FORMATION	

Account 4. Households and Private Nonprofit Institutions

Current Account

4.1	Consumption expenditure (1.5)	4.7	Compensation of employees (2.1)
4.2	Interest on consumers' debt −(2.8)	4.8	Income from unincorporated enterprises (2.2)
4.3	Direct taxes (5.10)		
4.4	Other current transfers to general government (5.11)	4.9	Income from property (2.3)
		4.10	Current transfers from general government (5.3)
4.5	Current transfers to rest of the world (6.5)	4.11	Current transfers from rest of the world (6.3*)
4.6	Saving (4.13)		
DISPOSAL OF INCOME		INCOME OF HOUSEHOLDS AND PRIVATE NONPROFIT INSTITUTIONS	

Capital Reconciliation Account

4.12	Finance of gross capital formation in noncorporate private sector (3.7)	4.13	Saving (4.6)
		4.14	Provisions for fixed capital consumption (1.2*)
		4.15	Net capital transfers from corporations (3.5*)
		4.16	Net capital transfers from general government (5.15)
		4.17	Net capital transfers from rest of the world (6.9)
		4.18	Net borrowing − (3.6 + 5.19 + 6.11)
DISBURSEMENTS		RECEIPTS	

(continued)

TABLE 2 (continued)

Account 5. General Government

Current Account

5.1   Consumption expenditure (1.6)
5.2   Subsidies −(1.4)
5.3   Current transfers to households (4.10)
5.4   Current transfers to rest of the world (6.5)
5.5   Saving (5.16)

5.6   Income from property and entrepreneurship (2.6)
5.7   *Less* interest on the public debt (2.7)
5.8   Indirect taxes (1.3)
5.9   Direct taxes on corporations (2.5)
5.10 Direct taxes on households (4.3)
5.11 Other current transfers from households (4.4)
5.12 Current transfers from rest of the world (6.3*)

DISPOSAL OF CURRENT REVENUE

CURRENT REVENUE

Capital Reconciliation Account

5.13 Finance of gross capital formation in noncorporate public sector (3.8)
5.14 Net capital transfers to corporations (3.5*)
5.15 Net capital transfers to noncorporate private sector (4.16)

5.16 Saving (5.5)
5.17 Provisions for fixed capital consumption (1.2*)
5.18 Net capital transfers from rest of the world (6.10)
5.19 Net borrowing − (3.6 + 4.18 + 6.11)

DISBURSEMENTS

RECEIPTS

Account 6. External Transactions (Rest of the World)

Current Account

6.1   Exports of goods and services (1.9)
6.2   Net factor income from rest of the world (2.10)
6.3   Current transfers from rest of the world (4.11 + 5.12)

6.4   Imports of goods and services −(1.10)
6.5   Current transfers to rest of the world (4.5 + 5.4)
6.6   Surplus of nation on current account (6.7)

CURRENT RECEIPTS

DISPOSAL OF CURRENT RECEIPTS

(continued)

TABLE 2 (concluded)

Capital Reconciliation Account

6.7 Surplus of nation on current account (6.6)	6.11 Net lending to rest of the world $-(3.6 + 4.18 + 5.19)$
6.8 Net capital transfers from rest of the world to corporations (3.5*)	
6.9 Net capital transfers from rest of the world to households (4.17)	
6.10 Net capital transfers from rest of the world to general government (5.18)	
RECEIPTS	DISBURSEMENTS

SOURCE: *A System of National Accounts and Supporting Tables*, Statistical Office of the United Nations, 1953.

NOTE: Numbers in parentheses indicate accounts and items of counter-entry in the accounts. An asterisk denotes "part of" item listed.

The old UN national income accounting system contains six inter-related accounts, but the last three of these accounts each have two separate parts, current and capital. The accounts are Domestic Product, National Income, Domestic Capital Formation, Households and Private Nonprofit Institutions, General Government, and External Transactions (Rest of the World Account). The first three of these accounts are con-solidated for the economy as a whole. The Domestic Product Account shows on the right-hand side the expenditures on gross domestic product, and on the left-hand side net domestic product at factor cost, capital consumption, indirect taxes, and subsidies. Income arising in the rest of the world sector is excluded, and the distribution of income to the various sectors of the economy is not shown. The National Income Account shows the income originating both in the domestic sectors and in the rest of the world, and how this income is distributed to the different sectors of the economy. The Domestic Capital Formation Account is consolidated for all the domestic sectors of the economy, showing on the left-hand side the gross domestic fixed capital formation and the increase in stocks, and on the right, the saving and financing of capital formation. The households and private nonprofit institutions sector, the general government sector, and the rest of the world sector all have both current accounts and capital reconciliation accounts. For all of these sectors, the current account shows receipts and outlays of a current nature, and the capital reconciliation account shows how saving, transfers, and borrowing finance gross capital formation.

The old UN system of accounts thus presents basically three types of account: production, current, and capital. There are three explicit sectors: households and nonprofit institutions, general government, and the rest of the world. In this system the rest of the world is treated as a sector rather than as an external transactions account, because it is specifically excluded from the enterprise sector with respect to both production and capital formation, and because like other sectors it is also provided with current and capital accounts. The definition of the household and nonprofit institution sector follows that already described for the United States. Although the coverage of the general government sector is the same as that of the US system, the old UN system considers that general government purchases of construction and equipment do constitute gross capital formation.

The structure of the old UN accounts is shown in Figure 2. The Domestic Product Account is a consolidated production account extending over all domestic sectors. The National Income Account is a current income and outlay account extending over both the domestic sectors and the rest of the world. The Domestic Capital Formation Account is a consolidated account extending over the domestic sectors, and for each of the explicit sectors of the economy a current income and outlay and a capital reconciliation account are provided, making in effect a nine-account system.

The New United Nations System

The Rationale of the Revision

In recent years there has been considerable pressure for revision of the United Nations System of National Accounts. The elaboration and extension of national accounting and the construction of disaggregated economic models have made it both possible and necessary to formulate a new system if international standards and reporting are to keep pace with the actual work being done in a number of different countries. The desirability of integrating input-output and financial transactions information with national income accounting data has been recognized for some time, and it is evident that the framework of balancing accounts could be expanded to do this satisfactorily. It is also

FIGURE 2

The Structure of the Old UN System of National Accounts

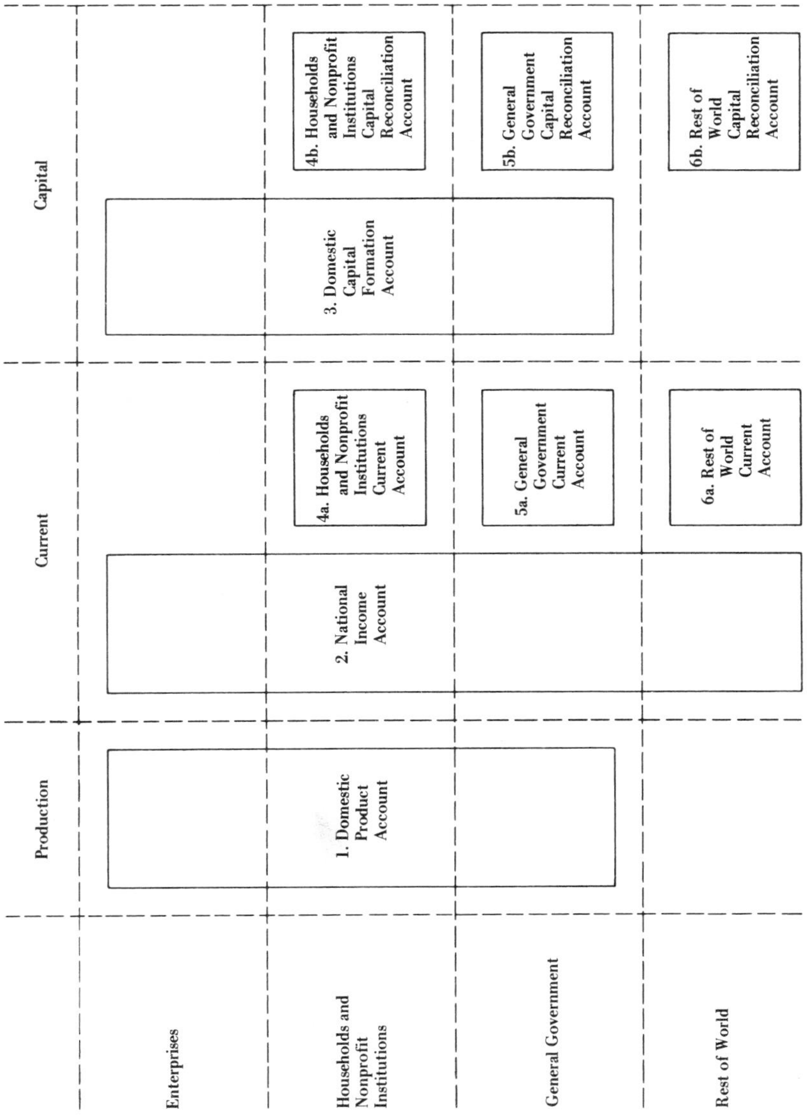

evident that an expanded system of national economic accounts is necessary to provide a consistent statistical picture of the development of an economic system, and in describing and analyzing economic change for many forms of economic decision making.

In 1964, an expert group of economists from a number of different countries was convened by the Secretary-General of the United Nations to consider the revision of the SNA. During the next four years a number of documents were produced. Special regional meetings were held in different parts of the world on different aspects of the proposed system. Use was also made of the studies and discussions of other special groups convened by the United Nations on such topics as constant prices, income distribution, and selected aspects of the structure, classification, and tabulations proposed for the new system.

The new UN system, its authors state, is not intended to represent a shift in emphasis; rather, by providing the necessary basic information in a more complete and comprehensive fashion, it seeks to modernize the system to take advantage of recent developments in statistical capabilities and to permit a wider range of problems to be studied. It explicitly recognizes that a national accounts system should provide a data framework for the collection of economic statistics, and that a properly constructed national accounting system can be used to test the consistency and adequacy of data coverage in many areas. The system is regarded as a target for statistical development, a target that will not be reached in the same degree or same manner by all countries. One of its major functions is to provide explicit links between complex representations of an economy and the simple, familiar national income accounts. Systems of consolidation are provided so that the masses of detailed information can be reduced to summary information for the economy as a whole. It is also expected that the revision will provide the basis for a revised system of international reporting, but the specific way in which this will be accomplished has not yet been detailed. Other related topics such as the development of national balance sheets, the distribution of income, the development of regional accounts, and the linking of the UN system to the material products system used by the Eastern European countries are also left to later development.

The Matrix Approach

The conceptual basis of the new UN system is a matrix approach to the classification of types of economic activity, sectoring of transactors,

TABLE 3

The New UN System: A Primary Disaggregation of the National Accounts, Including Balance Sheets

		1	2	3	4	5	6	7	8	9	10	11	12	13	14	15	16
Opening assets	1 Financial claims										1,249		165				
	2 Net tangible assets										661						
Production	3 Commodities				245	166		6	41			50					
	4 Activities			443		44											
Consumption	5 Consumer goods/purposes						210					2					
	6 Income and outlay			14	241						−19	13					
Accumulation	7 Increase in stocks										6						
	8 Fixed capital formation										41						
	9 Financial claims										58		18				
	10 Capital finance	1,217	693				27			59				−23	44	1,253	764
The rest of the world	11 Current transactions			51		2	12			17							
	12 Capital transactions	197	−32			1						1		0	−2	214	−33
Revaluations	13 Financial claims										−21		−2				
	14 Net tangible assets										42						
Closing assets	15 Financial claims										1,286		181				
	16 Net tangible assets										731						

NOTE: In the columns, opening and closing assets are balanced by opening and closing liabilities; and net tangible assets are balanced by net worth.

and classification of transactions. An example of this matrix approach for a larger system of national accounts, which embraces balance sheets as well as national income accounts, input-output, and financial transactions, is shown in Table 3, which is taken from the UN proposal.[2] The revised SNA does not include balance sheets, and therefore covers only that area of the table which is shown within the heavy black lines. The matrix is symmetrical in that the same items serve as row and column descriptors, and for any given row and its corresponding column the accounts balance. It will be noted that while Table 3 contains different types of accounts and different kinds of transactions, there is no indication of sectors. The new UN system does provide sector information, in terms of both industries and institutions; this detail is shown in the more expanded matrix given in Appendix C. In the more expanded version, for example, the capital finance account shown as row and column 10 in Table 3 is further broken down by (1) type of capital formation, (2) type of capital transfer, (3) type of financial asset, and (4) institutional sector. By use of these fairly general matrices, it is possible to describe any type of accounts, any system of sectoring, or any transaction classification. The UN emphasizes, however, that the matrix presentation is a conceptual device to illustrate the underlying structure of the system, and does not constitute the new system as such.

The Standard Accounts

In the construction of the standard accounts, the revision of the UN system focuses somewhat more than in the matrix on sectors, in order to exhibit the relationships among various transactors and activities. The list of accounts is shown below. The full set of accounts will be found in Appendix B.

List of the Standard Accounts in the New UN System

Class I Accounts—Consolidated Accounts for the Nation
  Account 1. Domestic Product and Expenditure
  Account 3. National Disposable Income and Its Appropriation
  Account 5. Capital Finance
  Account 6. All Accounts—External Transactions
Class II Accounts—Production, Consumption Expenditure, and Capital Formation
    Accounts
  A. Commodities—Accounts 1, 2, and 4

[2] See [3], Table 6, p. 30.

B. Other Goods and Services—Accounts 1, 2, and 4
   a. Sales by Nonprofit Services and Direct Imports of General Government
   b. Final Consumption Expenditure of General Government
   c. Final Consumption Expenditure of Private Nonprofit Institutions Serving Households
   d. Final Consumption Expenditure of Households
C. Industries—Account 1, Production Account
D. General Government Services—Account 1, Production Account
E. Services of Private Nonprofit Institutions Serving Households—Account 1, Production Account

Class III Accounts—Income and Outlay and Capital Finance Accounts
A. Nonfinancial Enterprises, Corporate and Quasi-Corporate
   Account 3. Income and Outlay Account
   Account 5. Capital Finance Account
B. Financial Institutions
   Account 3. Income and Outlay Account
   Account 5. Capital Finance Account
C. General Government
   Account 3. Income and Outlay Account
   Account 5. Capital Finance Account
D. Private Nonprofit Institutions Serving Households
   Account 3. Income and Outlay Account
   Account 5. Capital Finance Account
E. Households, Including Private Nonfinancial Unincorporated Enterprises
   Account 3. Income and Outlay Account
   Account 5. Capital Finance Account

There are three major classes of these accounts: Class I accounts are the consolidated accounts for the nation. Class II accounts are deconsolidations of the Class I production account into commodity accounts, showing the available supply and disposition of goods and services, and industry accounts, showing the origin of domestic production. The Class II commodity accounts cover production, consumption expenditure, and capital formation. The Class II industry accounts show the production of commodities and other goods and services. The Class III accounts are deconsolidations of Class I income and outlay and capital finance accounts into the same type of accounts for institutional sectors. There are thus six different basic types of accounts for economic activities. These are (1) production accounts, (2) consumption expenditure accounts, (3) income and outlay accounts, (4) capital formation accounts, (5) capital finance accounts, and (6) external transactions accounts.

The major sectors of the economy for which accounts are drawn up are (1) enterprises, (2) general government, (3) nonprofit institutions serving households, (4) rest of the world, and (5) households.

The enterprise sector is broken into four different sets of subsectors: (a) commodities, (b) industries, (c) nonfinancial enterprises, and (d) financial enterprises. Nonprofit institutions serving households are treated as a separate sector. Although the rest of the world never appears as an explicit sector it is implicit in the sectoring of the economy, since it is excluded from domestic production and domestic capital formation but it is part of the consolidated national income and outlay account and the consolidated external accounts. Since nonprofit institutions have been separated from households, the household sector contains only final consumers who neither produce goods and services nor engage in capital formation.

The structure of the types of economic activity and sectoring in the new UN accounts is shown in Figure 3. The Class I accounts are consolidated, and show (1) production for domestic sectors of the economy, and for all sectors, (2) income and outlay, (3) capital finance, and (4) external transactions. These are accounts labeled I1, I3, I5, and I6. Accounts IIA and IIB show the supply and use of commodities in the system: the commodities supplied by industries, general government, and nonprofit institutions are used for consumption expenditure and capital formation. The production of the economy in terms of industry and sector of origin is shown in accounts IIC, IID, and IIE. Finally, income and outlay and capital finance accounts are shown for nonfinancial and financial enterprises, the general government, nonprofit institutions, and households, thus completing the full set of accounts.

The set of new UN accounts is considerably more comprehensive than conventional national income accounts. The Class I accounts do constitute an abbreviated set of national income accounts, but since they are consolidated for the economy as a whole they do not show the intersectoral relationships. On the other hand, although the new system lays the basis for input-output tables and financial transactions by sector, it does not present this information as part of the system itself but expects the basic data to be provided in the supporting tables. Actually, the 19 standard accounts in the UN list somewhat understate the number of accounts required, since the commodity and industry sectors, even in the summary presentation, are conceived as sets of sector tables. The UN recommends a minimum of seven sectors for the commodity and industry accounts, thus resulting in a basic system of 31 accounts.

FIGURE 3

The Structure of the New UN System of National Accounts

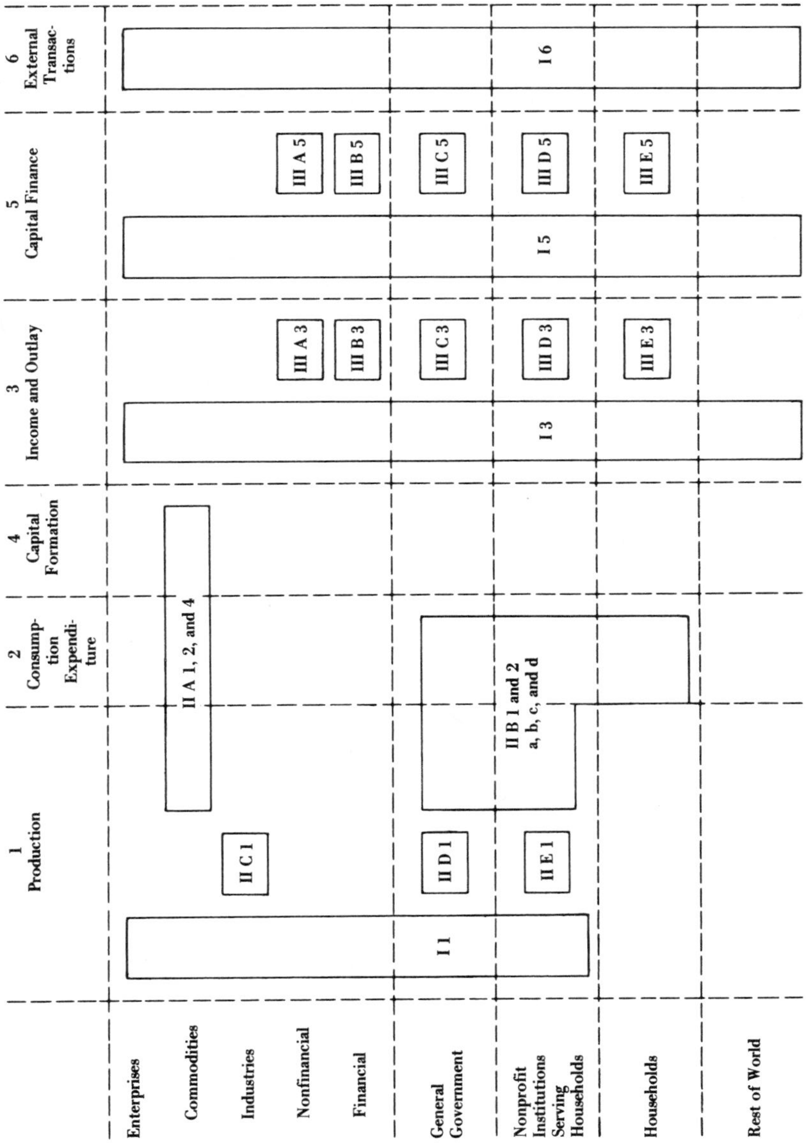

Evaluating the Structure of National Income Accounts

The three systems of national income accounts which have been examined cover four basic types of economic activity: production, income and outlay, capital formation, and external transactions. The revision of the UN accounts introduces two additional types of activity, consumption and capital finance, to provide data on the supply and use of commodities and on financial transactions. From the point of view of the national income accounting system, however, these do not constitute additional types of economic activity; rather, as is pointed out in the UN document, they are deconsolidations of the income and outlay and the capital accounts.

The division of the economy into sectors differs somewhat in the various systems. Nonprofit institutions are combined with households in the US and the old UN systems, but in the new UN system nonprofit institutions are shown as a separate sector. In both the UN systems, furthermore, a rest of the world sector separate from the enterprise sector is implicit. For the purpose of evaluating these systems, however, the discussion can be carried on in the context of the economic activities of three major sectors: enterprises, households, and government.

The Enterprise Sector Accounts

In none of the national income accounting systems examined is there an explicit enterprise sector. In the US and the old UN systems, the enterprise sector is consolidated with the productive activities of the economy as a whole. In the new UN system, the enterprise sector is included as part of the consolidated Class I accounts, on the one hand, and deconsolidated into a number of commodity, industry, and financial and nonfinancial enterprise subsectors, on the other hand. The US and old UN systems thus present a somewhat too consolidated view, but the revision of the UN system goes further than is desirable in the standard accounts toward deconsolidation. The enterprise sector is divided into so many subgroups that it loses its separate identity.

The enterprise sector should cover all of the market activity of the economy, both profit and nonprofit, carried on in the context of enterprises. Production carried out by the general government or by households that is not sold in the market should not be included in the output of the enterprise sector. If the government hires civil servants to produce public services that are not sold this constitutes nonmarket output by the government; the government is in fact providing services to the economy outside the market mechanism. Similarly, if an individual raises food for his own consumption, this is also output which does not reach the market sector. In less developed countries where the sub-sistence sector is large such household production may be important, and the national income accounts would accordingly show that a smaller share of the total output of the economic system originates as enterprise output.

The classification of private nonprofit institutions raises special problems. The US and the old UN systems include nonprofit insti-tutions serving households as part of the household sector, on the ground that these nonprofit institutions do provide free private con-sumption goods. The UN revision, however, recognizes that the activity of such organizations is not the same as household activity, and that the homogeneity of the household sector would be substantially im-proved by the exclusion of nonprofit institutions. The solution it adopts is to set up a completely separate sector for nonprofit institutions serving households. This means that this sector, like other sectors, must have a complete set of accounts and its transactions must be articulated with those of other sectors. This solution is not really satisfactory, however. In the United States the gross product of the nonprofit institutions that are included in the household sector was only $17 billion in 1966, out of a total gross national product of $743 billion. In other words, the nonprofit sector in the new UN system would repre-sent only 2.3 per cent of the US economy, and would have less analytic significance than many subsectors of the enterprise sector.

In a number of important respects nonprofit institutions do operate like enterprises; for example, a nonprofit hospital hires employees, buys materials, and charges patients in a manner quite similar to profit-making hospitals. The difference in legal form of organization does not appear to warrant setting up a completely different major sector of the economy. Merely because an operation is carried on in the enterprise sector does not imply that it is profit-making; government enterprises, for example, are included in the enterprise sectors of both the US and UN systems. In view of these considerations it would seem that the best solution is to include nonprofit institutions serving households as part of the enterprise sector, and to recognize that they provide free private consumption in much the same way that the government provides free public consumption.

The recognition of enterprise consumption provided by nonprofit institutions does suggest the further question of whether profit-making enterprises may not also provide free consumption goods directly to the public or to their employees. In the United States, for example, television and radio entertainment is supported by business advertising, but since neither the US nor UN systems recognize enterprise consumption as an economic activity these consumption goods are excluded from final output entirely. Yet in other countries where these same activities are supported by taxation they are considered to be a part of public consumption and thus are included in final output. In a similar manner, consumption goods that the enterprise provides to its employees as fringe benefits, such as recreation facilities, subsidized cafeterias, health clinics, expense accounts, etc., are not included in either employee compensation or consumer expenditures, yet such services do exist, and they are enjoyed as a part of the private consumption provided by enterprises.

It is therefore suggested that the activities of the enterprise sector should be shown much more explicitly than they now are in either the US or UN national income accounts. The role which this sector plays in the production of goods and services and the distribution of income generated by market activity, and the consumption which it provides through the operation of both profit and nonprofit institutions, should be fully reflected in the system of accounts. In particular this suggests that in the national income and product account the productive contribution of enterprises be distinguished from the production taking place in households and general government, and that an income and outlay account and a capital formation account be provided explicitly for the enterprise sector so that its role in the economy can be seen more clearly. Although the deconsolidations provided by the UN revision of the enterprise sector do provide much useful information, they would seem more appropriate considered as supplemental deconsolidation and sub-sectoring of the primary national income accounts.

The Government Sector Accounts

The definition of the government sector is generally the same for all the national income accounting systems examined. They all cover general government only, excluding the trading activities of government enterprises. The accounts provided for the government sector, however, differ considerably between the US and UN systems. In the US system all outlays by the government are considered to be current, and the government does not engage in capital formation. The UN system, however, does recognize expenditures on construction and equipment as capital formation by the general government. The UN treatment seems preferable, since it is logical to consider that government expenditures that provide a flow of services in future periods are capital formation just as are similar expenditures undertaken by enterprises. If this treatment is adopted, the flow of services arising from past government expenditures on capital goods must be included in government current consumption.

The Household Sector Accounts

As noted above, the US and the old UN systems of accounts have a combined household and nonprofit institution sector, but the new UN system excludes nonprofit institutions, thus considerably improving the homogeneity of this sector. If this procedure is followed, the question then arises as to whether the household sector proper engages in either production or capital formation. The US and the old UN systems include employees hired by the household, i.e., domestic servants, as part of the productive activity of households, but do not recognize any capital formation by households. Owner-occupied houses are treated as businesses; the flow of services they produce is treated as enterprise income, and their construction is considered capital formation by the enterprise sector. The purchase of consumer durables is considered current consumption expenditure. The UN revision does not recognize either productive activity or capital formation by households. Domestic servants, like doctors and lawyers, are considered to be self-employed, and thus are included in the enterprise sector; since the line of demarcation between self-employed persons who provide services to the household and employees of the household is quite arbitrary, this treatment seems logical. The treatment of owner-occupied houses in the new UN system is similar to that of the current US system, and purchases of consumer durables are again classified as current consumption expenditures.

If, however, enterprise activity is to be defined in terms of market activity, there are a number of productive activities that should be considered as taking place within the household. The household that grows food for its own consumption is engaging in productive activity that is not included in the enterprise sector; no market transactions are involved. In a similar manner, the flow of services provided by owner-occupied housing reflects current nonmarket activity taking place within the household, and when an individual purchases his own home he is in fact engaging in capital formation.

Furthermore, consumer durables do provide a continued flow of services within the household sector. Treating the purchase of an automobile, for instance, as a current consumption expenditure does considerable violence to the facts; some households retain them for periods ranging up to ten years or more, and during World War II it became obvious that the stock of automobiles was an important asset that was capable of yielding services over an extended period of time. One of the hallmarks of modern economic development has been the rapid growth in the production of consumer durables. Such consumer durables as dishwashers, refrigerators, stoves, and air conditioners are often included in the purchase price of the house to which they are attached, and they are often financed by the mortgage on the house. It does not seem reasonable to subtract from the value of the house the cost of the durable goods which are built into it, or to exclude them from capital formation on the ground that they have been purchased separately.

There is also another argument for considering expenditures on consumer durables as capital outlays. In the early years of a family's lifetime, expenditures on consumer durables (including such things as furniture) are likely to be particularly heavy. In contrast, retired persons spend relatively little in these categories. If the time distribution of the services of durables is not taken into account, the rates of consumption of families at different points in their life cycles will be distorted. It is true that the services of consumer durables do not produce monetary income and retired people do need monetary income for some purposes (e.g., Medicare) but the realities of the situation are that there are capital costs involved in setting up a household, and retired people are receiving a flow of services from the assets that they have accumulated during their lifetimes. In studying the development of the economy, furthermore, the accumulation of consumer durables over time by the household sector is, as has been shown by Juster in his study of household capital formation and financing [22], an important dimension of economic growth and development. If this form of capital accumulation is not taken into consideration, an important set of information relating to economic activity and behavior will be omitted.

In view of these considerations, it is suggested that the activities of the household sector include both production and capital formation, as well as consumption. The productive activity that takes place within the household should be entered in the consolidated production account for the economy; households should be provided with a capital formation account that would recognize both owner-occupied housing and consumer durables, and the flow of services of these owner-occupied houses and consumer durables should be included in household consumption.

Summary of Recommendations on the Structure of National Income Accounts

Both the US and the old UN systems of accounts were constructed to show the major flows of economic activity among the different sectors of the economy. Both systems have been quite successful in providing an overview of the operation of the economic system, and are widely relied upon for this purpose. The new UN system, however, does not serve this purpose as well. On the one hand, the consolidated accounts for the economy as a whole, i.e., the Class I accounts, do not contain accounts for sectors, so that information on the economic activity of government and households is not separately presented. The deconsolidation of the production, consumption, and capital formation accounts in terms of commodities, industries, nonprofit institutions, households, and general government, and the deconsolidation of the income and outlay and capital finance accounts for nonfinancial enterprises, financial enterprises, nonprofit institutions, households, and general government do contain the necessary intersectoral information, but at the cost of introducing a great deal of detail that is not required for an overview of the operation of the system, and that in fact interferes with an understanding of what is taking place. It has already been noted that the accounts listed on pages 26 and 27 and shown in Appendix B do not reflect even the minimum breakdown of the commodity and industry sectors that are recommended for the revised UN system. Even the full set of proposed national accounts, however, does not contain the detailed data required for input-output tables, flow-of-funds tables, etc. This information is presented in a set of 28 supporting and

FIGURE 4

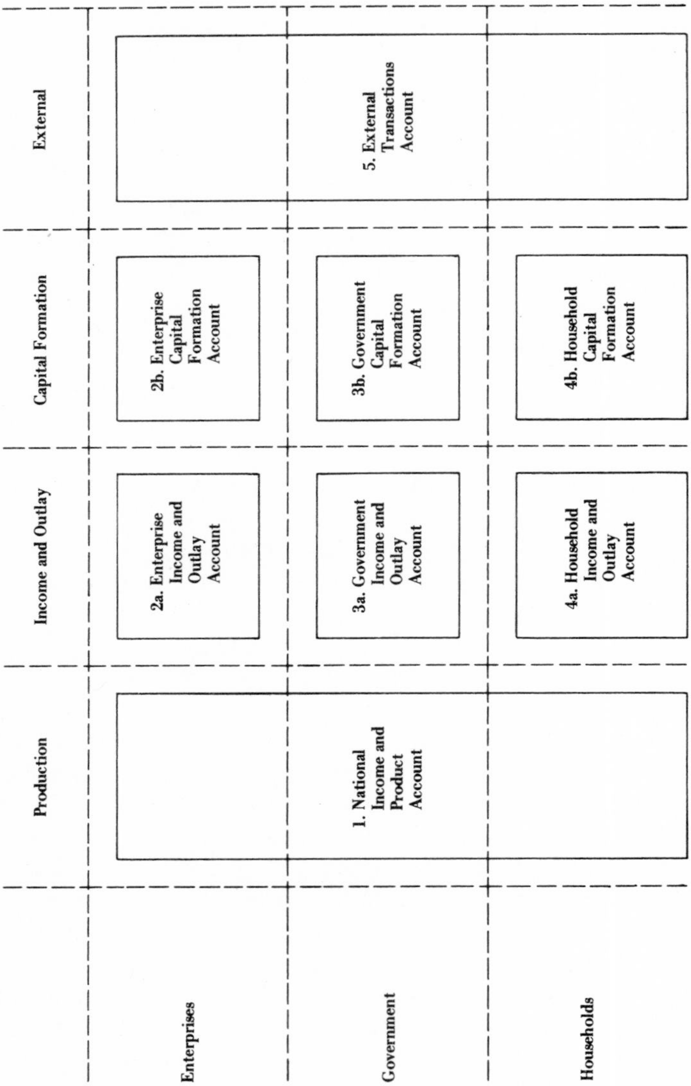

The Structure of the Proposed System of National Income Accounts

supplementary tables. The new UN system in its consolidated form thus provides too little information about the economic activities and the interrelationships of sectors, but in even the initial deconsolidation it provides such a complex and detailed network of flows that the relationships are obscured. It is therefore suggested that a level of deconsolidation approximating that contained in the US and the old UN systems should be retained.

Specifically, it is suggested that four economic activities (production, income and outlay, capital formation, and external transactions) and three sectors of the economy (enterprises, general government, and households) should be recognized. For productive activities and external transactions, it is further suggested that the activities of all sectors be consolidated to show the performance of the economy as a whole, but for income and outlay and capital formation, separate accounts should be provided for each sector. It is expected, of course, that in supporting tables the breakdown of production activities by industry and sector would be shown. Figure 4 presents the structure of such a national income accounting system.

This system bears a much closer resemblance to the US and the old UN systems than it does to the revision of the UN system. It provides for the explicit recognition of the enterprise sector with respect to both income and outlay and capital formation. Both the general government sector and the household sector engage in capital formation; but, since each sector is provided with a separate capital formation account, the capital formation of the different sectors can be identified. Finally, by including the activity of nonprofit institutions in the enterprise sector, the homogeneity of the household sector is improved without introducing a separate relatively unimportant sector into the system.

3 ECONOMIC CONSTRUCTS IN THE NATIONAL INCOME ACCOUNTS

For a national economic accounting system to be analytically useful, it must define and measure blocks of transactions that correspond to concepts with economic meaning. Economic constructs are such blocks of transactions. At the most aggregate level, economic constructs emerge as the major totals of the system, representing income and product. Within these aggregates, major components such as consumption, capital formation, and factor shares are useful constructs to show the structure and behavior of the aggregates. In the process of further decomposition and deconsolidation, the economic constructs provide the basis for alternative classification systems. There is thus a continuum between macroeconomic analysis and the related economic constructs at the most aggregative level and more microeconomic analysis and the related detailed classifications at the most disaggregated level.

The Scope of Income and Product

Marked changes in the concept of income and product have occurred as national income accounting has developed. National income was first conceived of as the total of the incomes of all the households in the nation, and as a consequence many of the early estimates were based upon estimates of the size distribution of income—the number of households in various income classes. Later, emphasis shifted to the measurement of income generated by various kinds of economic activity. At this juncture, estimates were made both by computing the income originating in each industry and by estimating the totals for the major types of payments to the factors of production such as wages, interest, and profits. Then, with the shift in emphasis to the final use of output, a commodity flow approach to the estimation of production was adopted, and the product of the nation was viewed in terms of total final expenditures at market prices. At each stage in the development there has been considerable controversy over the scope of income and product coverage, and how the total should be measured and valued.

This process of change and development in the economic constructs still continues. Recently, Kendrick [23] has made a number of recommendations for restructuring the national income accounts so that they will be more useful in analyzing investment and growth. A number of his specific recommendations are familiar in the literature of national accounts, but he has provided a more comprehensive and systematic coverage of the problems and has set them into a quantitative context. Much of the following discussion is based on Kendrick's work.

Unpaid Family Activities

One category of major concern to Kendrick is that of unpaid services provided within the family. A large part of the productive effort of the household consists, of course, of the unpaid services of the housewife. It has long been recognized that the shift of housewives from the home into the labor force involves substitution of market-produced goods and services for home-produced goods and services, so that the resulting change in total output may be overstated. There is considerable merit in this position, but the problem of measurement is formidable and any measure which is used is likely to be ambiguous. For example, women who enter the labor force may continue to provide much of the necessary housekeeping service. They may perhaps spend more of their leisure time getting household tasks done and husbands and other members of the family may also undertake additional chores, thus trading their leisure for more income. The question immediately arises whether leisure itself is not an output of the system, but the problem of valuing it is again very difficult. Kendrick also questions the omission of other unpaid services performed by households. For instance, individuals contribute time to such voluntary organizations as hospitals, welfare agencies, and political organizations. Students working in school are educating themselves, and in some sense are perhaps as productive or more productive than they would be if they had entered the labor force. Kendrick suggests that all of this unpaid productive activity might be valued in terms of its opportunity cost.

There can be no doubt that the household is involved in uncompensated productive activity, and to some degree existing national income accounting recognizes this explicitly by introducing estimates for food produced and consumed on farms and for imputed rent of owner-occupied housing. In less developed countries, identifiable economic activities such as the making of clothing or other household handicrafts have also been recognized in the national accounts. There are in addition a wide range of activities that fluctuate between the market and the nonmarket sector. Private transportation provided directly by the household for its own use undoubtedly represents one of the major productive activities of the household in the US economy. The fact that men shave themselves and many women do their own hair rather than going to barbershops and beauty parlors is again evidence of productive activity in the household.

The question of productive activity taking place within the household unquestionably needs further study. Time budget studies of how people divide their total time among different activities (including eating, sleeping, and leisure) would be highly informative, and would provide a valuable set of data that could be directly related to the market transactions in the national economic accounts. However, it does not now seem feasible to include a comprehensive coverage of all productive activity taking place within the household in the accounts themselves.

The Services of Durables

As noted in the preceding chapter, the treatment of durables owned by households, government, and enterprises also raises problems. An imputation is made for the services of owner-occupied housing, and it may well be asked why such an imputation is made for housing but not for the services of other consumer durables such as the appliances in the house and private automobiles. It was suggested in discussing the structure of the national income accounts that households do engage in capital formation, and that such capital formation should include the purchase of consumer durables. But if the purchase of consumer durables is treated as capital formation, durables must also be considered to yield a flow of services over time. The value of these services could be imputed on the basis of the cost of renting equivalent services, or alternatively what it costs to own the durable goods (i.e., a capital charge equal to capital consumption plus imputed interest). The research on household capital formation and financing by Thomas Juster [22] and other work going on in both the Department of Commerce and at the Federal Reserve Board [24] have indicated that it is quite feasible to make estimates of the contribution of the services of household durables to current productive activity, and it is therefore suggested that the scope of income and product measurement be expanded to include this element.

The treatment of durable goods owned by the government should parallel that of consumer and producer durables. The services of government-owned durables should be measured where possible by their equivalent rental value, or by the alternative of computing the costs of owning the durables. This treatment is necessary if comparability is to be maintained between the valuation of services in the general government sector and that in the enterprise sector. One of the major criticisms of many general government operations has been that their costs often do not include the total cost of the capital used, whereas the same operation carried out as an enterprise activity would include all costs. For example, a toll road operating on an enterprise basis would include both amortization and interest charges in the computation of the cost of providing services. The cost of providing public roads should similarly take into account not only the amortization of the capital cost of the road but also the fact that the roads represent a use of capital and thus involve an imputed interest cost.

Even in the case of business enterprises, problems arise in computing the cost of producer durables for national accounting purposes. Capital consumption allowances in the national accounts are largely based upon current business practices, which in turn reflect the tax laws. Such special tax regulations as accelerated depreciation, designed to encourage specific kinds of investment activity, distort the picture. So do price changes. Depreciation allowances are customarily based upon original cost and where prices rise significantly depreciation allowances based upon the lower prices of past periods may seriously understate the current value of capital consumption. In less developed economies, and even in some sectors of developed economies, businessmen may neglect to keep track of depreciation. In view of all these problems, the national income accountant is forced to estimate the value of the capital consumption actually occurring in the enterprise sector. The need for such estimation does not mean that the book value of the depreciation allowances charged for tax purposes is irrelevant; such data are an integral part of the transaction network. But they cannot be used alone as the basis for measuring the actual amount of capital consumed during a given period.

Development Expenditures as Capital Formation

In most existing national income accounting systems, gross capital formation is composed of final expenditures on tangible, reproducible goods. Intangible services are considered part of capital formation only to the extent that they contribute to the value of the tangible goods; thus, the services rendered by architects in the design of a building and paid for in the form of architects' fees are reflected in the value assigned to the building, and transportation, delivery, and installation charges of equipment are included as part of the value of the equipment.

There is a striking parallel between this concept of capital formation and the concept of output in general that is used in the material product system of the Soviet Union and the Eastern European countries. Actually, the concept of capital in the MPS and the western national income accounting systems is identical, and this concept of capital formation is essentially Marxist. The MPS system is thus perfectly consistent, in that its concept of capital matches its concept of output. Western national income accounting has recognized that intangibles and services do constitute current productive activity, but this recognition has not been carried over into the concept of capital.

In the study of economic development, however, there has been a growing realization that development expenditures for such purposes as education and health are major factors in economic growth, and for a society they constitute valuable intangible assets. For national income accounts purposes, it would be useful to classify development expenditures as capital formation for three reasons. First, in evaluating alternative allocations of an economy's resources, expenditures for roads and expenditures for education should be considered in the same terms of reference. It is a serious error to consider roads as capital formation merely because they are tangible, and education as not capital merely because it is intangible; the economy's efforts toward future self-improvement should be measured in terms of the resources devoted to both tangible and intangible capital formation. Second, in estimating the consumption in which a government or an economy is indulging, it is misleading to consider that all of the resources that do not result in tangible capital goods must necessarily represent consumption in the current period. In budgetary terms, the allocation between current use of resources and government capital formation intended to provide for future growth and development is significantly distorted if all intangible development expenditures are written off as current consumption. Third, there is a flow of services from the stock of intangible capital. Setting up the category of intangible capital leads to explicit recognition of this flow of services, and as a consequence both production originating in the government sector and total output will be increased.

It is particularly important to distinguish those expenditures that will have their primary impact on the growth and development of the economy in future periods for the government sector. In some countries, an appreciable part of the government budget is devoted to such purposes. To an increasing extent governments are aware of their obligation to make substantial improvements in the social and economic capital of their countries in intangible form, as well as the more tangible forms of roads, highways, parks, etc. It is somewhat questionable whether expenditures on national defense should be considered either intangible or tangible capital formation; by convention, military equipment is excluded from producer durables and it seems reasonable to write off military expenditures of an intangible nature as well.

Households may also make expenditures of a developmental nature. Kendrick, in fact, suggests that the rearing costs of children, the opportunity costs of students in the labor force, medical expenditures by households, and the mobility costs of families moving from one location to another all be considered intangible capital expenditures.[1] As regards society, Kendrick may be quite correct that many of these are development expenditures, but in relation to the individual household, it seems more reasonable to consider the cost of rearing children a consumption activity, from which families receive current benefits. The question of imputing opportunity costs for students has already been discussed; the general conclusion reached was that such an imputation, like the imputation for the opportunity cost of housewives' services, involved such complex problems and such a major departure from the current practice of reporting primarily market transactions that it should not be undertaken in the context of the national income accounting framework. Medical expenditures do have a future impact, but as in the case of rearing children much of the benefit may occur in the short

---

[1] See [23], p. 13.

run. Some types of preventive measures undertaken to promote future health, e.g., certain forms of dental care, inoculations, chest X-rays, etc., might well be amortized over time, however. Finally, mobility costs may in fact be either for current consumption or for future benefit, but it is difficult to distinguish those mobility costs which should be amortized over time and those which should be written off in the current period. Therefore, while in principle development expenditures for the household should be recognized, this category should probably be confined to direct outlays on education by households and certain limited classes of expenditures on health.

Enterprises also undertake development expenditures that are now written off as current expense. Thus, for example, businesses undertake research and development to improve products and to advance technology, and the cost of this research and development is written off as current expense. The cost of the training and education of employees is also generally considered current expense, though the benefit of such training and education to the firm and to the economy may continue in future periods as the employees contribute to economic activity. If the present contribution of past research and development and education and training expenditures equalled present outlays, there would of course be no significant distortion in the measurement of total economic activity. However, if these expenditures are increasing substantially there will be a systematic understatement of total economic activity, and also an understatement of profits resulting from current productive activity. It is also reasonable to assume that expenditures on research and development and education and training are sensitive to fluctuations in profits, so that failing to take them into account will distort reporting of cyclical fluctuations in economic activity.

If development expenditures of government, households, and enterprises are to be considered intangible capital formation, it will also be necessary to measure the flow of services yielded by this intangible capital over time. For some types of development expenditures such as education it is possible to consider that there is a given stock of education and training, physically embodied in the population and labor force. By appropriate demographic accounting techniques it would be possible to show how this stock of educated and trained personnel changes as newly trained individuals enter the labor force and older persons retire or die. For most intangible capital, however, the task is not so simple, and the amortization of the original expenditure over time inevitably possesses a certain degree of arbitrariness. Nevertheless, amortization over even a short period of time would be a substantial improvement over writing these expenditures off as part of current cost. Study of the process of research and development, furthermore, does provide some guide as to the impact of research and development expenditures over time. Some development work is short-run, oriented toward products which are already in the process of production. Other research may be long-run, intended to achieve results only after a long period. As in the case of tangible capital goods, the total flow of services from intangible capital should include not only the amortization of the expenditures, valued in current price terms, but also the proper interest cost.

The question remains whether the flows of services provided by intangible capital constitute net additional flows of services in the economy, or whether they are already fully embodied in existing flows. In the case of development expenditures by enterprises, it is generally assumed that these expenditures contributed to the income earned by the enterprise in the present period, and are thus already included in the income originating in the enterprise. However, to the extent that the development expenditures are basic research, which society as a whole can use to good advantage, a social product over and above the private product may well exist. Basic research carried out under government contract or provided by enterprises as a public service may be of this nature. Such research, like that of the government and nonprofit institutions, probably should be considered to yield a net flow of services over and above the income flows generated.

It would also be possible to consider that the services of past intangible expenditures of government and households were fully reflected in the income of the economy. Thus, past educational expenditures yielding a flow of present services could be assumed to be fully reflected in the higher incomes of individuals in the present period. In this case, however, it seems more reasonable to make the assumption that although past education does affect the level and distribution of income in the present period it has other major social benefits that are not captured in the compensation that individuals receive for their services. It is very difficult, furthermore, given the time lags and technological change, to estimate precisely what contribution past education expenditures are now making to present income. For this reason, it would seem somewhat more reasonable to consider that the flows of services of past intangible expenditures by both government and households do in fact constitute additional present income.

The Definition of Intermediate Goods and Services

The question of what constitutes an intermediate good or service in the economy has been at the heart of many national income accounting controversies. When the concept of the gross national product was first introduced, the question was raised whether the inclusion of all public expenditures on goods and services as final product did not result in double counting. If the government services are supplied to enterprises, it can be argued that such services are intermediate goods and services, which are fully reflected in the final output of the enterprises. But the problem of what is an intermediate good or service is not restricted to general government expenditure. A considerable portion of the expenditures of households could also be considered to be intermediate. An individual, for example, must commute to his job, and this expense can be considered an intermediate cost related to earning a living. Since clothes are bought to wear at work, and meals are purchased at work during the day, these too can be considered part of the cost of earning a living. This concept can be extended further. Many household expenditures are essentially of the nature of regrettable necessities, and are a part of the cost of living. Thus, an individual may live in a colder climate rather than in a warmer climate because of his job; the cost of heavier clothing and of heating his home might then be considered part of the cost of living in the colder climate. If the location of his job is such that he must live in a high rent community, the excess rent could be considered business expense. Even visits to his psychiatrist or vacations at luxurious resorts could be considered necessary expenses required so that he can continue to function at his job and earn income.

Thus, for both the household and the government sectors the line between intermediate and final goods is difficult to draw, and as a result current national income accounting practice has been to consider that almost all expenditures by households and the general government are final expenditures. Although this procedure does result in a grosser concept of output that may not correctly reflect the increasing costs of maintaining the society, it does nevertheless have the advantage that *all* the expenditures of households and the government are shown in the national accounts, so that the behavior of these sectors can be more easily analyzed.

The distinction between intermediate and final goods for the enterprise sector is of course basic to the concept of gross product originating in enterprises. In computing gross product for an establishment in the enterprise sector the costs of goods and services used in current production are deducted from the value of sales and change in inventories in order to arrive at a measure of value added. In developing the end use pattern of final output, national income accountants have used the commodity flow approach; this involves classifying each good or service produced in the economy either as an intermediate good or service used up in the process of production or as a final product used for consumption or capital formation by enterprises, households, or government. Any change in the definition of what is an intermediate or a final product would, of course, affect the measurement of total output. It has already been suggested that research and development expenditures and education and training costs of business be considered developmental expenditures by business, and thus a part of final goods and services. There are, however, additional current outlays by business which result in a flow of goods and services apart from those directly produced by the firm or industry in question. For example, in the United States an enterprise may, in order to advertise its product, support radio or television productions. Since advertising expenses are considered to be part of the current production costs of the enterprise, television and radio entertainment is classed as intermediate. In countries where the government pays for television and radio directly, however, these expenditures appear as public consumption and thus are counted as final goods. It does not seem reasonable that the particular form of support of the television industry should determine whether or not the output of this industry is an intermediate or final product. It is true that in the United States an individual in one sense pays for his television by listening to commercials, but this still does not alter the fact that the programs themselves in a very real sense constitute final output. Other mass media supported largely by advertising might also be considered to be final output. Thus, magazines and newspapers should be considered as final, rather than intermediate, products of the system. In those instances where advertising expenditures are undertaken purely for their own sake, e.g., billboards, direct mail, etc., they would of course not be final products.

Enterprises also write off as current expense goods and services that are provided to their employees directly as consumption goods. In large companies employees may receive as fringe benefits such things as recreational facilities, the use of medical clinics, subsidized eating facilities, and the use of expense accounts. If these benefits are provided to employees individually, it would probably be preferable to consider them payments in kind, and to consider the consumption good or service part of the consumption of the household. But when the goods and services are given in a more general form to a wider group of employees or to the public at large and the individual has little control over their supply or use, it would be useful to consider them to be enterprise consumption in much the same way that services provided by the government to the general public are considered to be public consumption.

In summary, there are strong reasons for enlarging the scope and measurement of national income and product to take into account (1) the services of durable goods owned by households and the general government, (2) the services of intangible capital created by expenditures of the government, households, and enterprises, and (3) the contribution of those goods and services currently written off as current expenditures by the enterprise sector that in fact are direct contributions to final output.

The Aggregates of Income and Product

National income accounting not only depends upon the definition of economic activity and the sectoring of the economy; it depends also on the creation of economic constructs around which the system can be built and which can be broken down in a number of different ways to show the structure and behavior of the system. The determination of the scope of the national income and product measurements is highly germane to the content of the economic constructs. But explicit consideration of what constructs should be developed and how the different constructs should be related to each other is essential.

National Income and Product Measures

Three major considerations enter into the development of measures of national income and product. (1) How gross should the measurement of output be? (2) Should the coverage refer to the residents of the country or to the activities taking place within the geographic area of the country? (3) Should output be measured in terms of market prices or in terms of the factor payments generated by economic activity? Each of these considerations gives rise to a different type of measurement, and as a result there are a considerable number of different national income and product measurements in current use.

Gross national and gross domestic product at market prices are the grossest measures of output now used. In countries where the residents receive a substantial flow of net income from abroad, the gross national product, which represents the total income and product of the residents of a nation, will be larger than the gross domestic product, which represents the income and product of the geographic area. On the other hand, in countries where residents of other nations share substantially in the ownership and operation of enterprises within the country there may be a net flow of income to other countries, and thus gross domestic product would be larger than gross national product. The US and the UN uses of these concepts differ somewhat. The US production account is built around the concept of gross national product at market prices, whereas the UN consolidated production account is built around gross domestic product at market prices. In the US system, gross domestic product is not shown explicitly anywhere, but the present UN system does show gross national product in its supporting tables. The new revision of the UN system also relies on gross domestic product at market prices as the aggregate measure of total output, and does not show gross national product.

Gross domestic product at factor cost, which is defined as gross domestic product at market prices minus indirect taxes net of subsidies, does not appear in the standard accounts of either the US or UN systems, but it is shown as the aggregate of gross product originating by industry in the supporting tables of the old UN system. In the new UN system, gross product originating by economic activity is shown both at market prices and at factor income, which is the same as factor cost.

The new UN system introduces a new net concept, disposable income for the nation. This is equal to gross national product at market prices minus the consumption of fixed capital. In other words, it is the net national product at market prices. This concept, which is shown as the total of the consolidated income account for the nation, replaces the concept of national income and the equivalent concept of net national product at factor cost that is used as the basis of the national income account in the old UN system.

In the US system, national income (net national product at factor cost) is presented as a subtotal in the national income and product account, and is used in supplementary tables as the total of income originating by industry and by sector and legal form of organization.

In summary, the new UN system has adopted gross domestic measures in its production accounts, and net national concepts for its income and outlay accounts. The valuation of the income and product aggregates is at market prices, and in fact the traditional concept of national income does not appear in the system. Furthermore, the emphasis on domestic product also means that the familiar concept of gross national product does not appear explicitly.

There has been a growing tendency in national income accounting to use gross rather than net measures of income and product. In part, the reason for this is that the grosser concepts provide an opportunity to include more data about the operation and functioning of the economy, and economists have in large measure given up the income and product aggregates as measures of economic welfare. If the scope of income and product measurements is to be further extended in the directions suggested above, the statistical difference between the gross and net concepts would be substantially increased. The capital consumption and amortization charges of the tangible and intangible capital of households, governments, and business enterprises would be very much larger than at present. The net measurements of income and product would increase only by the amount of the net imputed services arising from the inclusion of the additional tangible and intangible stock of capital. As regards the income and product system as a whole, the net concepts altered as proposed may be more meaningful measures of current income and output than the gross measures, so that the net measures may take on increased importance.

Personal Income Concepts

Personal income is the total income received by the household sector, including not only income originating from economic activity but also transfer payments. The US and the old UN systems have similar concepts of personal income. The treatment of social security contributions is not spelled out in detail in the UN system. In the US system social security contributions are split into two parts: that paid by the employer, and that paid by the employee. In computing the income received by employees, the US considers the employers' contribution a tax payment by employers to the government directly, and excludes it from personal income. In the new UN system total social insurance contributions are treated as a part of employee compensation, and are classified as a receipt of income and a tax payment by households. There is considerable logic to this treatment, since from the producer's viewpoint social insurance contributions are part of what he must pay to hire labor, and thus part of his total wage bill. In terms of actual payments, the employer not only pays the employer's share of the social security tax but also pays the employees' share and even withholds part of the employees' income tax and pays it directly to the government. From the household's viewpoint, take-home pay or even disposable income might be a more reasonable measure of income. As economic constructs, both personal income and disposable income are useful measures, and should be explicitly included in the national income accounting system.

Both the US and the old UN systems of national income accounts include the income and expenditure of nonprofit institutions in the household sector and thus in personal income. In the new UN system, however, nonprofit institutions are transferred into a separate nonprofit sector and are not included in personal income. On the other hand, if the scope of national income and product accounts is expanded in the manner suggested above, personal income would be increased substantially by the gross flow of services of the stock of consumer durables and development expenditures. The concept of gross personal income thus created would, in terms of grossness, correspond to the concept of gross national product for the nation. Such a new economic construct would be useful, since it would show the difference between the total flow of goods and services at the disposal of the individual and the net flow originating from economic activity and transfers in the current period.

Major Components of Income and Product

Besides aggregates, the national income and product account contains a number of major components. On the product side of the account, the two major components that are generally shown are consumption and capital formation. On the income side of the account there are three major components: factor payments, indirect taxes, and capital consumption. Factor payments include the compensation of employees, interest paid, proprietor and rental income, and corporate profits. Indirect taxes reflect the difference between factor payments and total income generated in terms of market prices. Capital consumption shows the difference between net and gross income and product.

Consumption

If the scope of national income and product is to be extended in the manner which has been suggested, the definition of consumption would change substantially. The flow of services resulting from the stock of past capital expenditures (both durable goods and development expenditures) for both households and governments would be included, but at the same time household and government current outlays on durable goods and development expenditures would be excluded. In countries where there is substantial economic growth, present outlays by households and government for durables and development expenditures generally exceed the flow of services derived from past expenditures, and as a result consumption under the new definition would tend to be substantially reduced.

The second major change in the definition of consumption is the introduction of enterprise consumption. To the extent that enterprise consumption consists of consumption by nonprofit institutions, it would merely result in a reclassification of some consumption from the household sector to the enterprise sector. However, if the suggestions made above concerning the inclusion of consumption services provided by business such as television, radio, and other mass media and fringe benefits for employees are adopted, a net increase in the consumption taking place in the economy as a whole would result.

In the US national accounts system, consumption for the economy as a whole is not shown. Personal consumption expenditure is shown, but for the government only total outlays on goods and services are presented with no division between current consumption and capital formation. Both the old and the new UN systems do explicitly recognize final consumption expenditures of households, nonprofit institutions, and the general government, but of course this definition includes as part of final consumption total current outlays on durable goods and development expenditures, and excludes the services provided by the stock of past expenditures. No recognition of enterprise consumption is made in either the US or UN systems.

Capital Formation

The extension of the concept of capital formation to include consumer durables and the development expenditures of households, governments, and enterprises will result in a substantially larger concept of capital formation than is customary in current national income accounting systems. Such an extension is necessary, however, if we are to gain an appreciation of the total amount of resources being devoted to the creation of the economic and social capital for future growth and development. This is important for economic and social policy, since in periods of emergency what appear to be reductions in current consumption by households and government, or what appear to be reductions in current costs by enterprises, may in fact merely be reductions in the purchases of consumer durables by households and in the outlays on development by government and enterprises. Such reductions would have repercussions in future periods since a smaller stock of consumer durables and intangible economic and social capital would be available for future growth and development.

The concept of capital formation in the US national income accounts is quite restricted. It is confined to private expenditures on structures, durable equipment, and inventories. No capital formation is recognized for either households or the general government. Both the old and new UN systems recognize capital formation of the general government, including structures, equipment, and inventory change, in a manner similar to enterprises. As in the US system, no capital formation is recognized for households; owner-occupied houses are considered a form of business enterprise. Neither the US nor UN systems take into account development expenditures by any sector, thus, as already suggested, adopting what is essentially a material product concept which defines capital in terms of tangibility rather than in terms of function.[2]

[2] Kendrick is engaged in developing time series beginning in 1929 for nonbusiness capital outlays, developmental expenditures for all sectors, imputed rentals on nonbusiness capital stocks, and business consumption and investment charged to current expense, in addition to the imputed value of unpaid labor services referred to earlier.

Factor Payments

The term "factor" is much abused in national income accounting. It originated in the theory of value, where it was used to indicate the existence of "factors of production" such as labor and capital. Early in the development of national income accounting it was recognized that when indirect taxes are levied on a product the market value of output includes not only payments to the factors of production but also the payments of indirect taxes. In order to differentiate between the market price valuations including indirect taxes and the resource cost of producing a given item, the term "factor cost" was introduced. If the economic system were purely competitive and all resources were completely mobile the concept of factor cost would have some validity, since it would represent resource use. But if the economy is not purely competitive the payments to the factors of production will not represent resource use, but will merely indicate the income payments which are generated by market forces. Thus, for example, if in a specific industry there exists a high level of demand together with monopoly, the factors used in that industry (both capital and labor) may receive payments that are large relative to the factor payments made for the same amount of resources used in other industries. The payments to the factors of production as they appear in the national income accounts, therefore, cannot be used as valid measures of resource utilization. In this sense, the term "factor cost" is a misnomer, and the more recent term "factor income" is a welcome change. In economic terms, "factor payment" might be more appropriate than either.

The analysis of types of income payments and the relative income shares of the factors of production, however, does not necessarily rest on the assumptions underlying "factor cost." National income accounting should be able to provide measurements to show how the factors of production share in the income generated by the economic system. Unfortunately, in many situations the returns to labor, capital, and entrepreneurial activity are combined in a single transaction flow. In enterprises such as farming or retailing, for example, the determination of factor shares on the basis of transactions information alone is not possible. The farmer or small shopkeeper, after paying all of his expenses, receives a residual net income that compensates him not only for his labor but also for the contribution of his capital, his entrepreneurial skill, risk-taking, or any other elements that might give rise to income. Customarily, official national income accountants have been hesitant to involve themselves in further analysis of this type of flow. But the accounts do provide the basis for making the imputations required to separate the various types of return.

Two basic methods of computing the labor contribution of proprietors are readily available. First, it could be assumed that proprietors in a given industry receive the same compensation per hour as do other employees of similar skill in the same industry. In the case of a farmer, for example, the compensation could be figured at the average that a farm manager or farm laborer would receive for an operation of equivalent size. Similarly, the imputed wage of a retail shopkeeper would be that of managers or clerks in equivalent-sized stores. This method of imputation essentially considers that the farmer or shopkeeper could earn a specific income if employed as a combined manager and laborer in the same industry, and that this opportunity cost can be used to value his labor contribution. A second method would compute the labor return as the residual remaining after payment of the other factors of production. Thus the farmer or shopkeeper could be considered to earn the amount left over after allowance was made for the return to capital in the enterprise. The use of a residual return for the imputation for either labor or capital implicitly assumes that the total contribution of these two factors is equal to the total income generated by production. It is quite possible, however, that the value of the labor and capital contribution in an enterprise will exceed the income generated, so that the enterprise should show a loss. Similarly, if the income generated exceeds the value of labor and capital resources used, the enterprise should reflect profit over and above the contributions of the factors. For this reason, it would seem preferable to impute the value of factor contributions in terms of opportunity cost. In countries where a large percentage of the labor force is self-employed it may be that the assumptions underlying the imputation would dominate the result to such an extent that the analysis of labor's share would not be meaningful. But in highly developed industrial economies where wage and salary payments predominate, the imputation of labor compensation for the self-employed has the advantage that it prevents the change in the relative compensation of the labor force over time from being dominated by the changing proportions of self-employed in the total labor force. It will still be useful, however, to distinguish between compensation of employees which is actually paid and that which is imputed for the self-employed.

With respect to the use of capital, a somewhat similar problem of imputation exists. If all capital were borrowed, the return on capital could be considered to be the interest paid for its use. However, many enterprises supply much of their own capital; the return on their equity is generally considered to be the residual left over after all other costs (including depreciation) are paid. Interpretation of profit rates among industries with different financial structures thus is quite difficult. For example, public utilities customarily borrow heavily to finance capital expenditures, and thus their equity represents a small part of the total capital they use. In contrast, large manufacturing firms obtain most of their capital by plowing back earnings, and their equity represents a large part of their total capital. The utility firms may have relatively low rates of total return on capital, but quite high rates on equity. Conversely, the manufacturing plants may have very high total rates of return, but their rates of return on equity may well be less than in industries where the funds used are largely borrowed.

Stigler solves the problem of comparing the rates of return on capital in different industries by adding together interest payments and profits, so that the rate of return on capital used by an industry will not be affected by the financial structure of the industry [25]. Implicit in such a computation, however, is the already discussed assumption that the total income originating in an enterprise can be divided between the factor payment to labor and the factor payment to capital. Furthermore, considering the total of interest payments and profits as a factor payment to capital provides a somewhat distorted view of the contribution of capital. Merely because capital is employed in a highly profitable industry, it does not necessarily follow that the contribution of capital is high. Monopoly, for example, may be highly profitable and provide a return to the enterprise over and above the contribution of either capital or labor. Profit may also arise from entrepreneurial skill or exploitation of labor, which results in underpayment of these factors of production. There would be considerable advantage in providing for a concept of net profit separate from factor payments to labor and capital. It would then not be possible to measure the factor payment to capital as a residual, and it would be necessary to provide a basis for imputation of the services of capital.

In developing an imputation for the services of capital in enterprises the same principle could be applied to capital as was suggested for the labor of self-employed proprietors. The gross contribution of capital could be valued at its opportunity cost, which in a competitive system would also be equal to its rental cost. Alternatively, an estimate of the contribution of capital (i.e., the capital charge) could be based on capital consumption (valued at replacement cost) together with a proper imputed interest charge. This basis of imputation is of course the same as that already discussed in connection with the flow of services from the stock of tangible and intangible capital in households and the general government. The detailed explanation of the actual imputations for the use of capital in both establishments and firms is presented in Chapter 6.

If the shares of capital and labor are thus computed, they may add up to more or less than the total of the income originating in the sector or enterprise. In fact, the concept of net profit is defined as the difference between the computed shares of labor and capital and the income originating in the enterprise or industry. Where net profits are high, this suggests that actual and imputed payments to labor and capital used in the industry do not absorb the total income generated in that industry. The explanation for this is not necessarily to be found in any single cause. It may be that labor is underpaid, a monopoly may exist, or there may be entrepreneurial returns not captured by the management. Furthermore, where net profit is zero it does not necessarily mean that the industry is competitive and is using its resources fully. It is quite possible for wage payments in the industry, for example, to siphon off what is essentially income due to monopoly elements, or for other stochastic elements to offset one another.

The question of what interest rate is to be imputed and whether different interest rates should be used in different sectors of the economy immediately arises. If the interest imputation is made on the basis of opportunity cost and the payment for risk and uncertainty relegated to the residual net profit, there are strong reasons for using a single interest rate throughout the economy. Furthermore, if the purpose of the imputation is to reflect the actual use of capital, the use of different interest rates in different firms or sectors makes it difficult to determine whether the capital return represents a payment for the use of capital goods or reflects a risk premium related to uncertainty.

Neither the US nor the UN systems of national income accounts provide for such direct measurement of factor payments. Proprietors' income is not divided between the compensation of the self-employed, the contribution of capital, and net profit. Corporate profits include the return to capital provided by enterprises together with the other residual profits earned. As they stand, the flows are not particularly meaningful, since shifts in the relative importance of the self-employed and changes in the financial structure of the economy do occur. The imputations that have been suggested for both the compensation of the self-employed and the contribution of capital would represent a step toward providing more useful and informative analytic constructs for the study of the differences among sectors and industries in the economy and their changes over time.

Indirect Taxes

The concept of indirect taxes has been one of the least satisfactory economic constructs in national income accounting. Generally speaking, the term "indirect taxes" serves as a catchall for all taxes that are paid by producers, with the exception of the corporate profits tax—the corporate profits tax is considered to be a direct tax on profits paid by producers.

The description of the nature and scope of indirect taxes provided in the new UN system indicates the extreme heterogeneity of the concept:

Common examples of the nature and scope of indirect taxes are import, export and excise duties, sales taxes, entertainment duties, betting taxes, business licences and transaction (e.g., stamp) duties, and real estate taxes. Real estate and land taxes are classed as indirect taxes except in those cases where they may be considered as merely an administrative procedure for the assessment and collection of income taxes. Also included among indirect taxes are levies on value added, the employment of labour and the use of fixed assets; duties in respect of the motor and other vehicles of industries and the services of general government and private non-profit institutions; and fees for driving tests and licences, passports, airport use, court and similar services paid by producers.[3]

From the standpoint of economic analysis, serious objection may be raised to the inclusion of many of these taxes as indirect taxes. Insofar as some taxes are in fact licenses and fees that represent payments for services provided by the government, they should be treated as purchases by businesses or households, and not as indirect taxes. In this connection

[3] See [3], p. 271.

it is interesting to note that one of the major differences in the measurement of private consumption expenditures under the US and UN systems is the difference in treatment of motor vehicle licenses and fees paid by households. In the US system these taxes are considered part of direct tax payments, and in the UN system they are regarded as indirect taxes. Still another alternative is to consider that motor vehicle taxes and licenses are fees that are paid for the operation of motor vehicle bureaus, and as such constitute a purchase of services by those desiring licenses. There is, of course, a real question whether the motor vehicle bureau provides any service to the individual other than giving him legal permission, or whether it provides the public good of general motor vehicle regulation. However, there are fees classified as indirect taxes that unquestionably do represent services provided to the user. Such fees as airport taxes and court fees are of this nature. By excluding these fees from indirect taxes they become intermediate goods and services for producers, thus causing the income and product originating in the firm to be smaller by this amount. For households, since the fees represent final consumption expenditures by households and sales of goods and services by the government, a greater portion of the total output of the government would be considered to be of an enterprise nature, and as a consequence the consumption goods provided by the general government would be smaller.

Taxes on the employment of labor also raise problems. The revised UN system is careful to include social security taxes in the compensation of employees and in direct taxes paid by households. As already noted, in the US system the employers' share of the social security contribution is treated as an indirect tax and the employees' share is treated as a direct tax, although both are paid by the employer directly to the government. It also seems somewhat inconsistent that the UN should recommend on the one hand that social security taxes be considered direct, but that other taxes on the employment of labor or the use of fixed assets be considered indirect. From an analytic viewpoint there seems little difference between a social security tax on wages and an employment tax on wages.

Finally, real estate and land taxes raise similar issues. A government wishing to tax economic rent will levy taxes on property, and in fact will be taking a portion of the share that is paid to this factor of production. If all real estate and property taxes fell on pure economic rent, there would be general agreement that such a tax is a direct tax on a particular factor share. However, a dilemma arises when the long-run incidence of taxes is considered. To the extent that property is reproducible, a tax on property in the long run would be the same as a sales tax on a currently produced item, and thus could be properly classed as an indirect tax. It is on the basis of such reasoning that the general view to date has been that property taxes can be considered indirect. The time has come, however, for a more serious analysis of this problem. A systematic study should be made to ascertain for various kinds of property classes the extent to which property taxes constitute an appropriation of economic rent by the tax system and the extent to which they represent a tax on reproducible capital. In this connection it should be borne in mind that a great deal of property even of the reproducible type has an extremely long life, and that although structures do not yield pure rent they do yield quasi-rent that can be directly affected by property taxes.

Capital Consumption

The concept of capital consumption has already been discussed in connection with the difference between the gross and net income and product. As has been indicated, the determination in economic terms of the amount of capital consumption that takes place over time presents substantial problems. The expansion of the concept of capital formation to include consumer durables and intangible capital for all sectors makes this problem more difficult. As in the case of indirect taxes, improvement in the measurement of this economic construct will require further investigation.

4 THE INTEGRATION OF NATIONAL INCOME ACCOUNTS WITH OTHER ECONOMIC ACCOUNTS AND RELATED DATA

Introduction

The evolution of economic accounting since World War II has made it evident that for many purposes the data contained in the national income accounts are too summary and consolidated. The development of other forms of economic accounts such as input-output, moneyflows, balance of payments, and program budgeting has for the most part occurred outside the national income. accounting framework. It has become increasingly evident to all concerned that an integration of all economic accounting systems dealing with related sets of transactions is essential, from the standpoint both of those generating the data and of those who wish to use it for economic analysis. The implementation of a large economic accounting system for a nation requires substantial resources, i.e., numerous statistical sources, specialized manpower, and computer facilities. Insofar as the various economic accounting systems deal with the same sets of data there should be considerable economy in developing all of the required estimates simultaneously. Decentralization of the task of estimation often results in duplication of effort, and inconsistency or noncomparability among similar parts of the related systems; from an analytic viewpoint, it confronts users with apparently conflicting sets of data, with no way to bridge the gap except through elaborate reconciliation tables that explain the conceptual and statistical differences.

In addition to the data contained in the formal economic accounts, supplementary and related sets of economic data are needed, such as further breakdowns of the major economic constructs, and prices or deflated value data that can be directly related to the economic accounts. The accounting system and the related economic data, furthermore, must be designed so that they can be directly related to social and demographic information. With the increasing amount of information required by different users, such as regulatory agencies, states, urban communities, and other groups concerned with special economic and social problems, the task of bringing system and order to the masses of information developed becomes more difficult, and the need becomes more pressing. Unless this can be done simply and easily it will not be possible to evaluate the operation of the economic system in terms of social goals, to analyze the impact of social change, or to examine proposed social policy in terms of the behavior of the economic system. In other words, the integration of the economic accounts with other economic, social, and demographic information is essential if we are to relate the operation of the economic system to the development of the society itself.

The integration of information systems depends in a fundamental sense upon the set of basic classification systems employed. Classification systems, like economic constructs, represent a method of grouping blocks of information having certain characteristics in common. As the social and economic systems change, so must the classification systems. For example, the industrial classification system of the twentieth century is quite different from that of a century earlier. The analytic models that are developed to study specific problems will in large measure determine the nature of the classification systems that are needed. Changes in knowledge and in theoretical approach will, therefore, also have major repercussions upon classification systems. However, the basic classification systems show substantial stability, and only change gradually over time. Those concerned with the design of classification systems must balance the need for new information against the need to provide continuity over time.

In this context, it is useful to examine the US and the new UN systems of national economic accounts to see to what extent they provide the basis for an integrated system of economic and social information. One of the outstanding characteristics of the US system is continual expansion of the amount of information provided, so that today it represents one of the most comprehensive sets of economic information available anywhere. The new revision of the UN system also has as a major objective the development of a framework into which the major forms of economic accounts can be integrated and which can provide the required basic information about the operation of the economic system.

The Integration of Economic Accounts

Over the last decade a consensus has been developing about the preferred method of integrating the various forms of national economic accounts. When the UN system was first adopted, this problem had not yet arisen. However, with the further development of data for the analysis of interindustry relations, financial transactions, economic planning, government budgeting, and the balance of payments, many countries and international organizations have become deeply concerned with the problem.

In the 1958 revision of the US national income accounts, the Department of Commerce seriously considered how the national income accounts could be integrated with other forms of economic accounting in the future. It was noted that the national income accounts could be deconsolidated to provide a framework for input-output tables and for financial transactions accounts. The subsequent work on input-output by the Office of Business Economics has followed this approach, and more recently the Federal Reserve Board has integrated the flow-of-funds accounts with the national income accounts. A general outline of a possible system of deconsolidation that would provide integration of all economic accounts (including national wealth and balance sheets) was presented in the National Accounts Review Committee Report [17], which appeared in 1958.

The new UN system also uses the principle of deconsolidation of the four summary accounts for the nation as a whole to provide a set of national economic accounts covering input-output and financial transactions, and to suggest a blueprint for the later integration of national wealth and balance sheets. Actually, the new UN revision presents not so much a system of national income accounts as such but rather a set of more general economic accounts that, with further deconsolidation, can present the additional sets of information required for different kinds of economic analysis.

The process of deconsolidation involves the development of classification systems that can provide the kind of information required. Each different form of economic accounts has its own classification requirements. Some of the types of classification systems will be very different, e.g., input-output tables and financial accounts, but similar classification systems may be used for related forms of economic accounts. Thus, for example, the classification used for input-output should be directly related to that for capital formation accounts, and the classification used for financial transactions, to that for balance sheets. An examination of each of the forms of economic accounts will indicate the types of classification systems that are required and how they are related to the problem of providing for an integrated set of economic accounts.

Input-Output Tables

Input-output tables are a deconsolidation of the income and product accounts of the nation. They show the value of products produced by specific industries in terms of (a) their inputs from other industries and their use of factors of production, and (b) their sales to other industries and to various final users. Since the focus of interest in these tables is on the technological relationships of the production and the demand for specific commodities, the industry and commodity classifications involved are developed to provide as much homogeneity as possible for both production and demand considerations. But there is a conflict between these two criteria. To analyze demand, industries should be specified in terms of homogeneous sets of commodities, without regard to whether they are produced by the same or different establishments. To analyze production functions, however, it is desirable to view the production process as taking place within specific productive establishments, each of which has a labor force, plant, and equipment, and may produce a variety of different commodities that from a demand standpoint might be classed in different industries. For this purpose, the industry classification of the establishment is based upon the general type of industrial activity in which it is engaged. The majority of input-output tables attempt to reconcile these conflicting criteria as best they can, but generally they provide information on an establishment basis.

As already indicated, the Office of Business Economics has published an input-output table that represents a deconsolidation of the national income and product account. However, this table does not represent a complete integration of input-output with the national income accounts, since the classification of industries in the two systems differs somewhat. Both industry classifications are based on the United States

Standard Industrial Classification System, but they differ in coverage. For example, the input-output table presents considerably more detailed classifications for manufacturing and less detail for the service industries. It, therefore, becomes difficult to relate the input-output data to the data on income originating by industry.

In the new UN revision, the input-output table is separated into two tables. The first shows the supply of commodities by establishments in the different industries and the use of these commodities. The second shows the use of commodities and the factors of production by establishments in different industries. Since the same commodity and industry classification systems are specified for input-output data and for the income and product accounts, the new UN system would result in full integration between these accounts.

Financial Transactions

In the United States, the flow-of-funds data provided by the Federal Reserve Board are now directly related to the national income and product accounts. The same major economic constructs, such as gross national product, gross domestic investment, personal income, consumer expenditures, and government expenditures, appear in the flow-of-funds accounts and in the national income accounts, in precisely the same form and with precisely the same values. Additional economic constructs such as gross national saving, gross national investment, and gross personal saving that are introduced by the flow-of-funds system are systematically related to the other constructs in the accounts. Basically, the flow-of-funds statistics show the sources and uses of funds by sectors and subsectors of the economy. The sectoring must, of course, be of an institutional nature, since those involved in financial transactions must by definition exist as legal entities. The integration of the detailed sectoring of the flow-of-funds data and the income and product data is not complete. Although the institutional subsectors of the two systems are directly related, they differ substantially in the amount of detail they provide. In the flow-of-funds subsectoring, particular attention is given to financial institutions; in the subsectoring of the national income accounts, the corporate and noncorporate sectors are broken down into broad industrial groups. More comparable subsectoring of the two systems would be desirable so that data showing the impact of financial institutions on the functioning of the economy and the financing of capital formation by major industrial sectors could be more fully presented.

The new UN revision includes income and outlay and capital finance accounts for each of the institutional sectors in the economy. These two accounts together provide the same information as the sources and uses sector of the Federal Reserve Board's flow-of-funds accounts. The capital finance account is further broken into two parts, one showing gross investment and its financing, and the other showing the net acquisition of financial assets and the related net incurrence of liabilities plus net lending. In essence, aside from the question of institutional sectoring, the new UN system adopts the same conceptual approach to integration as the US flow-of-funds.

Other Forms of Economic Accounts

The integration of other forms of economic accounts is less developed because generally they have not been as clearly formulated as either input-output or flow-of-funds. It seems clear, however, that national wealth accounts and balance sheets must be directly related to the changes in assets and liabilities information in the financial transactions accounts. This is recognized explicitly in the financial asset and liability accounts that the Federal Reserve Board provides for the US, and it is also shown in the extended matrix presentation in the new revision of the UN accounts. However, there are still major problems with both tangible and intangible capital assets and national wealth.

Efforts have also been made to integrate the national income accounts and government budgets in the United States. On the one hand, program categories have been introduced into the classification of government outlays in the national income accounts, and on the other, there has been considerable progress in changing the basis of government budgeting to the concepts used for national income accounting. The new UN revision explicitly provides for a breakdown of government outlays by purpose as well as by type of transaction. Further development of program and project budgeting and further deconsolidation of the national income accounts into institutional as well as program categories will provide a better integration of government budgets and national income accounts.

　　　Finally, balance of payments accounts are closely related to the external transactions account in the national income accounts. However, to use the balance of payments to make projections for the future or to understand what has taken place in the past, it is not only necessary to integrate the foreign transactions account with the national income accounts, but also to show data for the rest of the world explicitly in the deconsolidations of other accounts. For example, the input-output table must show the relationship of imports and exports to the domestic supply and use of goods and services. The rest of the world also needs to be treated as a subsector of the economy in the financial transactions accounts, and for certain types of assets and liabilities, domestic assets need to be distinguished from foreign assets. In other words, the national economic accounts must show how foreign transactions relate to the operation of domestic sectors, and in the majority of cases it is useful to show the gross foreign transactions taking place rather than just the net changes. The foreign transactions account itself requires further deconsolidation to show relationships with different areas of the world and countries. Because of the role of specific international financial institutions (e.g., the International Monetary Fund and the World Bank) and special kinds of transactions (e.g., special loans or grants), the classification system here may be somewhat different from that provided in the domestic financial transactions account.

Integration With Related Economic and Social Data

The formal national economic accounts are the systematic presentation of data on transactions (actual and imputed) for the national economy. For many kinds of analysis, however, such data are not sufficient. The rather highly developed and articulated system of national economic accounting must be related in operational terms to other forms of economic and social data, such as prices, quantities of output, regional data, and social and demographic characteristics.

　　　Integration of related economic data involves further elaboration of the device already used to integrate the national economic accounts. Specifically, the technique of deconsolidation and disaggregation of major economic constructs and summary economic accounts can provide the basis for developing related information at the different levels of aggregation.

Constant Price Data and Price Indexes

Since the system of national economic accounts reports transactions data, the major economic constructs are measured in terms of the actual prices at which they take place. A time series of the major economic constructs relating to output will therefore reflect both changes in prices and changes in quantity. The economist wishing to analyze the behavior of the economic system is very much concerned with separating the price change from the quantity change. As a consequence, almost every country that provides national income accounts also provides some of this information in the prices of a fixed base year so that quantity changes can be isolated.

The usual constant price data are for expenditure on gross national or gross domestic product at market prices. This breakdown purports to show the changes in real personal consumption, real public expenditures, and real capital formation. The constant price data are obtained by deflating the current expenditure data for specific goods and services by appropriate price indexes, or in some cases by using direct quantity measures for the changes in particular categories of goods and services. It is generally recognized that the measurement of expenditures at constant prices is a difficult problem, however. New products are introduced and old products undergo quality changes that cannot be measured. In the case of some services, e.g., those provided by many government employees, it is not possible to measure the quantity of output, so that input, measured in terms of the number of employees or hours of work, must be used as a substitute. As a result, for many sectors the constant price data reflect inputs, imperfectly measured, rather than outputs.

Output can also be measured in terms of the industries in which it originates. For this purpose it is usually desirable to deflate both the cost of goods and services that a given industry purchases from other industries, on the one hand, and the sales made by the industry, on the other. This double deflation method requires knowledge of the inputs into each industry and their prices, as well as the prices of each industry's output. In other words, the double deflation method must be carried out at a disaggregated level on the basis of input-output relations.

The problem of integrating price information into the national accounts is discussed at some length in the new revision of the UN system. It notes that the use of different bases (Laspeyres and Paasche) for price information results in different measurements, and that the specific formulation of the price index also is a matter of some concern. It also discusses the possibility of extending price index measurements over space as well as over time, deriving quantitative differences in the level of output by industry and by type of good among different countries. The problems here are even more formidable than those of comparisons over time, however, and the task of providing consistent and reliable price measurement encounters serious difficulty where there are wide differences in the patterns of consumption and in technology.

Since price index data are useful only to the extent that they can be related to existing economic constructs, national economic accounts provide a framework into which price information can be classified; in fact, most countries provide supplementary data tables showing the implicit price measurements that result from dividing the computed constant price data into the current price data. Such concepts as the wholesale price index or in many countries even the consumer price index do not have much conceptual validity if they are constructed outside of the national economic accounting framework. Often, for example, the wholesale price index is composed of a collection of miscellaneous items weighted in an impressionistic manner, so that the index has little economic significance; or the consumer price index may refer to a market basket of goods that is not relevant to any actual social or economic group of consumers.

Further Breakdowns of Economic Constructs

For many purposes the accounts for the nation as a whole provide information that is too aggregative to be useful. If, for example, one wishes to examine what is occurring within one region of the economy, or to compare the development in one region with that of others, the aggregative national accounts do not help. To the extent that the national economic accounts are built up on the basis of data gathered regionally, such as income tax data, social security data, economic census data, and data from regulatory agencies, regional information can be developed fairly easily from the national data. A considerable duplication of effort would be involved if each region tried to develop its own economic accounting data. Furthermore, if regional accounting data are not derived as breakdowns of the general national economic accounts, analysis of regional behavior cannot be analytically related to the operation of the national economy as a whole. In some cases, the national economic accounts do not provide sufficient detail for regional breakdowns, or do not contain the kind of information required, e.g., trade between regions. In these cases, data outside the national economic accounting system may have to be obtained, either on a sample basis or from other statistical sources. In order to provide a unified economic accounting system, however, such information must be tied directly to the regional breakdowns of the economic constructs provided at the national level.

Beside regional breakdowns, other kinds of breakdowns may also be needed. For example, there is considerable interest in the size distribution of income of households and individuals. To be analytically useful, the size distribution of income must also be fitted into the constructs of the national economic accounts relating to the household sector. The size distribution of income should be viewed as a tabulation of personal or disposable income by size class; other statistical sources may be required to generate such data, but the over-all context within which the data are developed should be consistent with the constructs and definitions of the national economic accounts.

For other major kinds of data, such as that relating to capital formation or government transfer payments, special breakdowns that provide additional information will be required. In such cases, deconsolidation and disaggregation are again employed so that the additional information fits within the general framework of the economic accounts.

The development of extensive breakdowns providing masses of information for regions, industries, subsectors, size classes, etc., has resulted in the publication of a tremendous volume of detailed data, but additional cross tabulations and more detailed breakdowns are still needed for specific purposes. On the other hand much of the mass of published detail is valuable only as reference material. Quantitative work involving the further processing or analysis of large amounts of published data requires that such data be put into machine readable form for the computer. In recent years, however, the published data themselves are the product of computer processing, and in many instances may even be direct computer printouts. In these cases, a considerable extra cost is involved if the data are published in printed form and the user must then put them back into machine readable form. Government agencies have recognized that the provision of machine readable information directly to users may in many instances be more satisfactory than publication of highly detailed data in printed form. As the detail and complexity of the data provided by the information system increases, the alternative of supplying specialized data in machine readable form will become more compelling. Those engaged in the study of regional economic development, for example, will want complete machine readable sets of data relating to particular regions. Similarly, in the case of an input-output table, the publication of a large matrix of 200 by 200 industries does not provide data that are particularly useful or manageable; a computer tape containing the basic input-output data is much more useful to those engaged in such analysis. Even the flow-of-funds data on financial transactions published at the level of greatest detail on a quarterly basis find relatively little use, but this same data in machine readable form can be used for a wide variety of analyses.

Published data should be in two categories: first, summary presentations leading to a broad understanding of the structure or behavior of the major elements that are being portrayed; and second, detailed listings of reference type data. Thus, for example, the *City and County Data Book* provides a number of pieces of economic and social information that those interested in a specific community can consult. In this particular instance, any one individual may be concerned with only a small part of the total data structure, but presumably there are enough individuals interested in different parts so that the publication of such reference data is useful.

The Integration of Social Data

To some degree social data are implicit in the structure of the national economic accounts. The distinction between households, governments, and enterprises is social as well as economic. The breakdown of transactions by type is often based on the social rather than the economic characteristics of the transaction, and the designation of regions and cities introduces further information of a nontransaction nature. Within the national economic accounts, social data are most relevant to the household sector. Here it would be useful to provide groupings of households not only by economic characteristics, such as the size of income, but also by social characteristics. Thus it is possible to distinguish individuals on the basis of race, age, education, and sex, and to discuss the character of a household in terms of the composition of the social characteristics of its members. Tabulations and cross-tabulations of the social characteristics of households, e.g., retired population, racial groups, education levels, family size, etc., can be provided. But this approach, if carried to the length which is in fact required for social and economic analysis, tends to be self-defeating. Dividing data into more and more cells by cross-classification soon reaches the point where the number of cells greatly exceeds the number of possible observations. Thus, for example, a consideration of households in each community in the United States by the characteristics of each of the households can rapidly lead to tabulations in which the number of cells exceeds the number of households in the United States. From an analytic point of view such a result is obvious, since the full set of characteristics for each household is in some real sense unique. In the past, attempts to resolve this problem have resulted in the production of a few summary tabulations that shed light on some problems but are quite inadequate for a wide range of other problems. A proper cross-tabulation for one purpose is often useless for other purposes.

A more promising method of integrating economic and social data is the creation of special sets of microdata. For many sets of aggregate data it is possible to establish a representative sample of individual reporting units showing the microdata on which the aggregates are based. For example, for the household sector of the economy it should be possible to construct a sample of households such that the total of the incomes of all households, weighted by the appropriate sample weights, would be equal to the total personal income for the economy as a whole. If the sample is representative, a distribution of the individuals in it by occupation and industry would yield the employee compensation paid by industry. Similarly, a distribution of the sample by size of income would yield the size distribution for the personal income sector as a whole. If the reporting unit in the sample is the household, demographic and social information about each household can be included. The composition of the household in terms of age and sex, education, occupation, and work status of each member can be provided, as well as what is essentially the household's complete income statement and balance sheet indicating such things as the nature and amount of income received, expenditures and saving, home ownership, possession of durables, etc.

An initial start in this direction has been made by the Bureau of the Census in their 1-in-1,000 sample of the US population. This sample contains information on approximately 100,000 households, and contains over 40 items of information for each household. The existence of a large sample of the household sector not only permits special purpose cross-tabulations to be made, but it also provides the basis for analyses involving simulation of household behavior. It is possible, for example, to extract from the household sample a specific group of households and examine through the process of simulation precisely how they and their behavior might be expected to change over time, under certain assumptions and in accordance with the past behavior of similar households. An example of such a simulation using the 1-in-1,000 sample of the population was carried out by James Schulz in order to investigate the economic circumstances of the aged in the year 1980 [26]. He developed a stochastic life process model that provided for the sequential aging of those members of the US population who were 40 years and older in 1960. The model involved applying mortality data, information on job turnover, ownership of private insurance, coverage by private pension plans, and eligibility for social security to individuals according to their characteristics. In applying mortality data, for example, the probability of a specific individual's death was based on the age, sex, and race of that individual, and whether the death actually occurred was determined by this probability and by the generation of a random number. Thus, if the probability of death for a specific individual was determined to be 4 chances in 1,000, a random number from 1 to 1,000 was generated, and if this happened to be 4 or less, a death was considered to take place. By applying this method of generating changes, a complete life process model was simulated for each individual in the sample for a twenty year period, bringing the time period up to 1980. A census of the sample was taken as of that date to determine the distribution of income and the economic circumstances of the aged. The major purpose of the simulation was not to provide a forecast or projection as such, but rather to test the sensitivity of the simulation to various changes in policy variables or structural shifts that might occur over the next 20 years.

The use of microdata relating to a sector or subsector of the economic accounts is not necessarily confined to simulations using demographic and social data. Joseph Pechman has used a microdata set of 100,000 tax returns, which represents a sample of those individuals who are subject to income tax, for analyzing the direct effects of changes in the income tax law [27]. In this type of analysis the individual tax returns for each taxpayer in the sample are processed under the various alternative tax regulations. An analysis of the differences that would result from the various regulations in terms of the total tax yield and the relative burden on different groups of taxpayers is then possible.

Other samples of microdata have been developed by private organizations. For example, Standard and Poor currently produces computer tapes containing quarterly financial reports of many of the major firms in the United States [28]. A wide variety of survey material is collected by both academic and commercial institutions. For the future integration of economic and social data it is important that on the one hand the national economic accounts be designed so that they can be implemented for certain sectors at the sample survey level, and that on the other hand those collecting sample survey information be encouraged to do so within a proper sampling frame and in a manner such that it can be directly related to the more general framework of economic and social information for the nation as a whole.

The Role of the Computer

The development of the computer in the last decade has made the processing of masses of information possible. Within the next decade it can serve as the basis for integrating economic and social data. Basic to such an integration, however, is the underlying framework of economic accounts and standardized classification systems for both economic and social data. The information system must be capable of yielding at the same time major economic constructs aggregated for the system as a whole, and highly disaggregated basic data. In particular, given the computer, it becomes feasible both to create and to use microdata sets which form representative samples of parts of the economic system and of society. The generation of the underlying disaggregated data and microdata sets is not difficult. The operation of many agencies of the government generates such information automatically. The Internal Revenue Service, the Social Security System, Motor Vehicle Registration Bureaus, and a multitude of other governmental operations automatically provide masses of information that can be utilized directly to provide the basis of the statistical system.

There is, however, a major problem of privacy and disclosure. In part, this problem has already been faced by governments in the collection of census information on individuals and establishments and records on crime and health. Before the advent of the computer, the major safeguard to privacy was the inability of the system to handle and process information and to collate information from different sources. Some federal agencies have been aware of the problem of confidentiality, and have refused to disclose their records even to other agencies or other parts of the government. Thus, for example, the Bureau of the Census is protected from having to disclose any of its records to Congress, and does not even provide to the Internal Revenue the names of individuals or companies from whom it obtains information. Archives has a long record of sequestering specific documents from the public and certain classes of documents from government agencies. Other operating agencies have not been as concerned with confidentiality of data, however. Security agencies have been able to obtain a wide variety of records from both public and private sources about the activities of individuals and companies, and people are naturally somewhat uneasy that a central statistical system containing individual data might be used against them.

Such fears seem entirely justified, and indicate the need for developing a system of safeguards. The entire problem of confidentiality of all data obtained by the government and by major private organizations such as credit agencies, major employers, hospitals, educational institutions, etc., needs to be considered explicitly. In many cases, the information collected by certain groups, public or private, may be considered improper and not in the public interest, and in other cases provisions should be made for specific safeguards. The development of safeguards of information is not new. The confidentiality of communication between a patient and his doctor or a lawyer and his client is protected to the extent that the courts cannot have access to it. The outlawing of certain types of reporting and eavesdropping is also being recognized.

The desire to provide against the abuse of data, however, should not go so far that data important for the analysis of economic and social policy are not collected or preserved. Social and economic information is essential in evaluating the effect of specific policies. For example, major questions of the desirability of urban redevelopment, the extension of equal opportunity, or alternative forms of education are all matters of national concern. Unless information is available for appraising such questions, those responsible for the design and implementation of policy will have no basis for judgment, and the social scientist cannot carry out an effective program of research.

The computer can help make possible the analysis of highly disaggregated and microdata while at the same time insuring confidentiality. In the majority of cases, the social scientist can request a specific form of data processing and ask the computer not for the individual data but for the results of the analysis. From the analyst's viewpoint, this is desirable and efficient, since by drawing on a central data file of highly disaggregated information he can obtain access to information in machine readable form without having to handle or process the information himself. Remote consoles will enable individual users to use central data files directly, and the confidentiality safeguards can be programmed into the system so that no information of a confidential nature will be released to any user. Specific operating agencies, of course, must have authorized access to certain kinds of information. The police, for example, should have access to information on what automobile license numbers are related to what owners—information to which, of course, they currently do have access. Merely because one group has access to certain information does not mean that others must or should have similar access. The question of who is authorized to have access to what information is a matter of major political concern that should be considered explicitly agency by agency, and should not be left to chance—or inefficiency.

5 CLASSIFICATION
SYSTEMS
AND INTEGRATED
ECONOMIC
ACCOUNTS

The integration of economic accounts requires that standardized classification systems be developed so that the data in the different parts of the economic accounting system can be directly related. The development of major economic accounting constructs does provide a general framework for the classification systems, but further deconsolidation of the accounts requires explicit consideration of a number of different interrelated classification systems.

In analyzing the integration of economic accounts, four different types of classification systems emerge as central. First, classification of products and industries is necessary, not only to show the origin and use of income and product, but to provide the basis for input-output tables, capital formation accounts, and balance sheets. Second, institutional sectoring of the economy is required to show how different kinds of enterprises, governments, and households allocate the income that they receive, and engage in financial transactions. Third, asset and liability classifications are needed for national wealth and balance sheet accounts. Finally, classification systems are needed for the various activities of governments, showing receipts in terms of types of taxes and outlays in terms of the economic nature of outlays and purposes for which such outlays are made. It should be emphasized that although these four systems of classification are different in purpose and coverage, they are highly interdependent, and should be developed in conjunction with each other.

Product and Industry Classifications

The classification of products and industries represents the most detailed and complex of the classification systems developed for economic data.

Considerable resources have been devoted to the development of such classification systems, by both the United States and the United Nations. It is beyond the scope of this discussion to evaluate or to suggest major revisions in either the US or the UN systems. It will be useful, however, to indicate some of the problems that must be borne in mind in the use of these classification systems for purposes of economic accounting.

Commodities

The classification of commodities into product groups is basic to the development of product and industry classification systems. Even the finest commodity classification is an aggregation, and the items that it embraces will differ from one another in discernible ways. How fine to make the commodity classification depends both on the importance of the particular commodities being classified and the magnitude of the differences among the commodities that are to be included in a commodity group. Commodities are differentiated on the basis of both the processes of production they involve and the uses to which they are put, and later aggregation of the basic commodity classifications may be either in terms of industrial activity or in terms of end uses. For the United States, the basic commodity classification is a 7-digit code, which collapses into a less detailed 5-digit commodity code, and into industry codes at 4-digit, 3-digit, and 2-digit levels. For the new UN revision a 3-digit classification is used, which embraces over 10,000 products and activities. The UN system is also telescoping, so that 2-digit major groups and 1-digit divisions of the economy are shown. At the present time, the UN International Standard Industrial Classification is being revised. The commodity classification for the national accounts will be based on the links between the subgroups of the Standard International Trade Classification and those of the ISIC. Although the Standard International Trade Classification provides a fairly detailed classification of commodities involved in international trade, it will be necessary to develop categories for other goods and services to obtain a complete commodity classification.

Industries

Although the commodity classifications can be grouped into broader industry classifications, and the output of the economy can be shown in terms of such industrial classifications, it does not follow that the activity of individual establishments and/or companies can be fitted into these industries. Some establishments produce a number of commodities that in the classification system are considered to be output of different industries. As a practical matter, establishments are classified in that industry that fits the largest share of their output. In analyzing the gross product originating on such a basis, however, it will be found that for any given industry composed of a given set of establishments, output will contain a certain proportion of commodities that in terms of the commodity classification belong in other industries, and conversely the total output of commodities that would be classified as belonging to a given industry will not be produced by establishments appearing in that industry.

As has been mentioned already, the treatment of input-output relations in the new UN system explicitly recognizes this problem. A dual classification is provided that shows on the one hand the supply of commodities produced by establishments classified in various industries, and on the other the commodity inputs used by establishments in different industries. From an analytic viewpoint, this distinction is very useful, and becomes more relevant as diversification within establishments becomes wider and the economic system becomes more complex. However, at major levels of aggregation most establishments do not seriously overlap into more than one category. Much of the apparent diversification in the economy comes about not at the establishment level but rather at the firm or enterprise level. In many ways, as plants become automated they may become more and more specialized and easier to classify. Publishing highly aggregated data both on the supply and use of commodities and on the gross output and input of industries may not be worthwhile, since at the published level of detail the differences between these systems of classification will not be significant; for input-output tables showing about 50 industries or less a single system of classification may be sufficient. For highly detailed data showing several hundred industries the distinction between establishment and commodity classification is pertinent, but here the mass of detail is so large that it should be handled in machine readable form. Ideally, one would like to have the distribution of specific products by kind of establishment within each industry group in this form.

The problem of industry classification becomes much more serious when companies rather than establishments are classified by industry.

Just as an establishment may produce a variety of different commodities that belong in a variety of industries, so a given company may own establishments in different industries. There are indications that this development may in the future make distributions of company activities by industry much more difficult. The US Census Bureau has recognized this problem explicitly, and has provided special studies on the nature of the industrial diversification of various companies. This evidence suggests that classification of companies by industry is only meaningful at fairly aggregative levels and that the more complex distributions of company-establishment activities will need to be provided in some machine readable form.

The company-establishment relationship is important not only in determining the industrial structure of the company, but also in analyzing the activity of the establishments themselves. To an increasing extent central offices of multiestablishment enterprises are taking over establishment functions, thus eroding the concept of the establishment and posing a problem of how central services are to be allocated to productive activity. There has been a growing tendency to pull administrative and research personnel out of the establishment and centralize them. The computer and modern communication systems permit accounting, design specification, customer relations, billing, and even payroll to be done by the central office. If the central office is considered a separate establishment, and charges are made for the services rendered on an internal bookkeeping basis, the central office function can be treated as a purchase of goods and services by one establishment from another. On the other hand, to the extent that the central office provides joint services to all establishments that are paid for out of the operating surpluses as a whole, the internal bookkeeping may not be relevant and it may be difficult to identify the industries using such services.

End Use

Commodities produced by the economic system flow into a variety of end uses. Individuals purchase goods and services to satisfy their various consumption needs. Business firms purchase durable goods for capital formation, and the government draws upon goods and services for both public consumption and capital formation. The task of providing data on the commodity flow is substantial, but it is undertaken by many countries so that the estimates of output by industrial origin will be consistent with the estimates of expenditures for final products.

Both the US and the new UN systems present quite detailed classifications of the goods purchased by consumers. The types of classifications involved are similar to those used for consumer budget studies. Both systems use a dual classification that distinguishes durability as well as purpose. Thus, for example, the purchase of automobiles and gasoline would both be shown under private transportation expenditures, but automobiles would be classed as a durable good, and gasoline as a nondurable good.

End use classifications for producer durables and government expenditures are also needed. These should correspond to the classification of assets and liabilities and the classification of government activities discussed below.

Institutional Subsectoring

The industry classification systems discussed above are based upon the analysis of economic activity in terms of products and production processes. For many purposes, however, it is necessary to view economic activity in terms of decision-making units: groups that have legal forms of organization and play a major role in determining the transaction flows in the economy. Such subsectoring of the economy for the analysis of income and outlay flows and capital transactions is quite different from the industrial classification used to analyze productive activity; it reflects institutional rather than technological characteristics, and is based upon the recognition of income recipients and ownership units. Only individuals and legally recognized entities can receive income, engage in financial transactions, and have balance sheets.

In presenting data for the United States, the OBE uses the following general institutional classification:

> Business
>> Corporate
>> Sole proprietorships and partnerships
>> Other private business
>> Government enterprises
> General government
> Households and nonprofit institutions
> Rest of the world

National income originating is shown for each of these major institutional sectors classified into compensation of employees, interest, profit, or other income arising from the sector. For some components (e.g., profits and income of unincorporated enterprises), the OBE also provides a further breakdown of the corporate and noncorporate sectors of the economy into 16 broad industry groups. For government, receipts and expenditures accounts are shown separately for the federal and the state and local levels.

The Federal Reserve Board has developed a related but somewhat more specialized institutional sectoring for presenting information on financial transactions, as shown below.

NONFINANCIAL
  Rest of world
  General government
    US government
    State and local government
  Private domestic nonfinancial
    Households
    Nonfinancial business
      Corporate
      Noncorporate
        Farm
        Nonfarm
FINANCE
  Banking system
    Monetary authorities
    Commercial banks
  Nonbank finance
    Savings institutions
      Saving and loan associations
      Mutual savings banks
      Credit unions
    Insurance
      Life insurance
      Other insurance companies
      Private pension funds
    Finance not elsewhere classified
      Finance companies
      Security brokers and dealers
      Open-end investment companies
      Agencies of foreign banks
      Banks in US territories and possessions

Although the Federal Reserve classification matches the OBE major sectoring, the detail presented differs substantially. The FRB does not provide any breakdown by industry of the corporate nonfinancial sector, and similarly the OBE does not provide the detailed financial sectoring of the economy.

The basic approach of the new UN system to institutional sectoring for income and outlay and capital finance accounts is similar, as shown on the following page.

Nonfinancial corporate and quasi-corporate
Financial institutions
General government
Private nonprofit institutions
Households, including private nonfinancial unincorporated enterprises

The major differences between this and the US system are that even in the basic income and outlay accounts the distinction between financial and nonfinancial enterprises has been introduced, private nonprofit institutions have been removed from the household sector, and private nonfinancial unincorporated enterprises have been placed in the household sector. To a considerable degree these differences arise because the revised UN system provides capital finance accounts for all the sectors for which income and outlay accounts are provided. Like the OBE, the new UN system provides industry detail within the institutional sectoring for some 23 industries. Households and private nonfinancial unincorporated enterprises are further broken down to show agriculture, nonagricultural unincorporated business, employees, and persons in other status. Under general government, additional detail is given for central, state, and local governments, social security funds, and other public institutions.

As in the US flow-of-funds accounts, the UN shows additional detail for financial institutions. The institutional subsectoring used for financial transactions accounts is shown below.

I. NONFINANCIAL ENTERPRISES
   Private
   Public
II. FINANCIAL INSTITUTIONS
   Central bank
   Other monetary institutions
      Private
      Public
   Insurance companies and pension funds
      Private
      Public
   Other financial institutions
      Private
      Public
III. GENERAL GOVERNMENT
   Central government
   State and local governments
   Social security funds
   Other institutions
IV. PRIVATE NONPROFIT INSTITUTIONS SERVING HOUSEHOLDS

V. HOUSEHOLDS
    Proprietors of nonfinancial unincorporated enterprises included in
       the sector, except owner-occupied dwellings
    Employees
    Persons in other status
VI. REST OF THE WORLD

Both the US and the revised UN systems thus exhibit apparent conflicts in the institutional sectoring of the economy for purposes of analyzing the generation and allocation of income, on the one hand, and the financing of capital formation and the role of financial institutions, on the other. For analyzing income flows, industrial elements must be introduced into the institutional sectoring to show how important different sectors of the economy are in the generation of income and to examine the rates of profits that are being earned. But financial institutions as such may be relatively unimportant since they generally are not major income producers. The sectoring of the OBE is directly oriented to this purpose. To analyze financial interrelationships, however, considerably greater detail has to be provided for the financial sectors, as has been done by the Federal Reserve. Unfortunately, the greater detail provided by the OBE in terms of institution and industry is not carried over into capital formation or financial transactions accounts, so that the financing of capital formation by the major producing sectors of the economy cannot be analyzed. For example, the financing of capital formation in the public utility, contract construction, and corporate manufacturing sectors differs considerably, and an understanding of the operation of the economy requires information of this type.

The UN system more fully meets this objective, since the institutional-industry sectoring that it develops for its income and outlay accounts also provides information on capital finance for the same sectors. The expansion of the UN system for the analysis of financial transactions is considerably more limited than that provided by the Federal Reserve Board, and in these accounts the nonfinancial sector is split into only two subsectors, private and public. Insofar as financial transactions are directly related to the allocation of income, the financing of capital formation, and the changes in balance sheets, it would seem more appropriate to provide considerably greater subsector detail for the financial transactions accounts of nonfinancial enterprises.

With respect to the treatment of the household sector, it does seem appropriate that nonprofit institutions should be excluded from the household sector; but the inclusion of unincorporated nonfinancial enterprises as part of the household sector should be seriously questioned. It is, of course, difficult to separate the household account and the enterprise account of an unincorporated enterprise. However, such a separation has already been made on the production side of the current accounts for unincorporated enterprises. Purchases of goods and services for operating the business have been separated from household expenditures, and unincorporated income has been computed as the income of the business accruing to the household. It does not seem unreasonable that the financial transactions and even in some degree the balance sheet of the unincorporated enterprise can be separated from the household accounts. For example, the owner of a small grocery store has as assets of his business an inventory of goods for sale and an accumulation of accounts receivable from his customers, and as liabilities accounts payable to wholesalers and perhaps even a note on his accounts receivable held by the local bank. Under such circumstances it is possible to compute an equity in the business that is obviously an asset to the owner of the business in his household capacity. This kind of separation of accounts in terms of the balance sheet is not significantly different from the separation that national income accounting makes on income and product account.

If both nonprofit institutions and unincorporated businesses are excluded from the household sector, the latter should reflect only individuals in their household capacity; it would probably be useful to introduce economic and demographic breakdowns somewhat along the lines suggested in the proposed UN system. Farm and nonfarm households of proprietors should be distinguished, as well as wage earners, professionals, and even the retired population. Although additional detailed socioeconomic groups would be useful for particular problems, it is probably true that microdata sets for the household sector could more easily provide the necessary information for finer subgroups.

In summary, therefore, a system of institutional sectoring combined with broad industrial sectoring is required for income and outlay accounts, capital formation accounts, financial transactions, and balance sheets. Furthermore, in order to provide for the analysis of the role of financial institutions in the system, the institutional sectoring will have to be expanded to show the various types of monetary and financial institutions. In order to analyze socioeconomic groups, the household sector should be restricted to individuals in their household capacity, and major subgroups should be shown.

Asset and Liability Classifications

The classification of assets and liabilities is directly related to the product classifications used for national income accounts, the capital formation and capital stock accounts used for input-output, the financial transaction accounts, and balance sheets. Since neither the present US system nor the revised UN system provides for capital stock accounts or balance sheets, complete asset and liability classification systems have not been drawn up in either of these systems. Nevertheless, parts of the classification do exist in the national income accounts and the financial transaction accounts.

There are three broad classes of assets: (1) nonreproducible assets such as land and natural resources; (2) reproducible assets, which are created as part of capital formation in a specific period; and (3) financial assets, which by definition also represent liabilities for some other sector or group. Nonreproducible assets are not classified by either the US or UN systems. That portion of reproducible goods that consists of structures and producers durable goods is shown. For the United States these categories are spelled out in some detail, as shown in Table 4. The detail of this classification is in marked contrast with that of the new UN system, which is given below.

> Residential building
> Nonresidential building
> Other construction
> Land improvement and plantation
>   Land improvement
>   Plantation, orchard, and vineyard development
> Transport equipment
> Machinery and other equipment
>   Agricultural
>   Other
> Breeding stock, dairy cattle, etc.

The importance of information on capital formation and capital stocks strongly suggests that the UN classification system needs to be substantially expanded. Much of the detail on structures will automatically be provided by the industry or institutional sector detail into which the various forms of accounts are broken down. With respect to producer

TABLE 4

The US System: Department of Commerce Asset Categories

Purchases of structures by type
  Private structures
    Residential structures
      New construction
        Nonfarm dwellings
          New dwelling units
          Additions and alterations
          Nonhousekeeping units
        Farm buildings
      Brokers' commissions on sale of
      structures
      Net purchases of used structures
    Nonresidential structures
      New construction
        Nonresidential buildings, excluding farm
          Industrial
          Commercial
          Religious
          Educational
          Hospital and institutional
          Other buildings
        Public utilities
          Railroads
          Telephone and telegraph
          Electric light and power
          Gas
          Other
        Farm
        Petroleum and natural gas well drilling and exploration
        All other private construction
  Public structures
    New construction
      Buildings, excluding military
        Residential
        Industrial
        Educational
        Hospital
        Other public buildings
      Highways and streets
      Military facilities
      Conservation and development

    Other public construction
      Sewer systems
      Water supply facilities
      Miscellaneous public construction
    Net purchases of used structures
Private purchases of producers durable equipment by type
  Purchases of new equipment
  Dealers' margins on used equipment (except passenger cars)
  Net purchases of used equipment from government
  Less: Exports of used equipment
       Sale of equipment scrap (except passenger cars)
  Furniture and fixtures
  Fabricated metal products
  Engines and turbines
  Tractors
  Agricultural machinery (except tractors)
  Construction machinery
  Mining and oilfield machinery
  Metalworking machinery
  Special-industry machinery, n.e.c.
  General industrial, including materials handling equipment
  Office, computing, and accounting machinery
  Service-industry machines
  Electrical machinery
    Electrical transmission, distribution, and industrial apparatus
    Communication equipment
    Other electrical equipment
  Trucks, buses, and truck trailers
  Passenger cars
  Aircraft
  Ships and boats
  Railroad equipment
  Instruments
  Miscellaneous equipment

durables, however, the redundancy of the classification system is much less obvious, since it is necessary to show even specialized types of equipment such as aircraft separately so that within an industry one can distinguish among the various forms of capital goods.

Since neither the US nor the revised UN system treats durable goods held by consumers as capital formation, these classifications will be found in the final consumption expenditures of households. Both the US and UN classifications seem to be quite satisfactory, and can serve as a basis for the classifications needed for the capital formation accounts and the balance sheets.

As to government assets, the US system recognizes public con-struction, shown in Table 4, but treats the purchase of durable goods by the government as current expenditure. There is no classification of durable goods purchased by the government in the US accounts. In the UN accounts, the same classification for type of capital goods is used for government as for other producers. In principle, this approach seems quite proper, but the classification might have to be expanded somewhat to include specialized government structures and durables (e.g., high-ways, dams, etc.).

For financial assets and liabilities the classification system will in large part depend upon the legal and institutional characteristics of the particular country involved. The financial asset and liability classification used by the Federal Reserve Board is shown in Table 5. The extent of detail shown here does facilitate the analysis of financial conditions. A much more abbreviated list of financial assets and liabilities is shown in the following new UN system.

Gold
Currency and transferable deposits
   Monetary institutions' holdings
   Central government's holdings
Other deposits
Bills and bonds, short term
Bonds, long term
Corporate equity securities, including capital participations
Short-term loans, n.e.c.
   Between monetary institutions
Long-term loans, n.e.c.
Net equity of households on life insurance reserves and on pension funds
Proprietors' net additions to investment of nonresident quasi-corporate
   enterprises
Trade credit and advances
Other financial assets

TABLE 5

The US System: Federal Reserve Board Financial Transaction Categories

Monetary reserves	Corporate and foreign bonds
Gold	Corporate stocks
Official foreign exchange position	1-to-4 family mortgages
IMF gold tranche position	Other mortgages
Convertible foreign exchange at	Consumer credit
Treasury and Federal Reserve	Instalment
Treasury currency	Noninstalment
Deposit claims on financial institutions	Bank loans, n.e.c.
Demand deposits and currency	Other loans
Private domestic	Open market paper
US government	Dealer-placed paper
Foreign	Directly placed finance company
Time deposits at commercial banks	paper
Savings accounts at savings institutions	Bankers' acceptances
Insurance and pension reserves	Other claims
Life insurance reserves	Security credit
Pension fund reserves	Owed by brokers and dealers
Credit market instruments	Owed by others
Consolidated banking items	Taxes payable
US government securities	Trade credit
Direct and fully guaranteed	Equity in noncorporate business
Short-term	Miscellaneous
Other except savings bonds	Deposit claims
Savings bonds	Equities
Nonguaranteed agency issues	Insurance claims
Loan participation certificates	Unallocated claims and bank floats
State and local obligations	Sector discrepancies

In its more detailed presentation the UN does provide sector breakdowns within these asset categories, but it does not provide any finer classifications of asset types. Although the major classifications of the revised UN system are generally satisfactory for purposes of international comparison, the different institutional and legal arrangements in particular countries will result in considerable difference in the detailed financial asset and liability classifications.

Classification of Government Activities

Three major types of classification systems are required for government economic activities: first, taxes classified by type; second, the outlays of the government classified by types of expenditure, i.e., purchases of

TABLE 6

The US System: Government Receipts Categories

Federal government receipts	Death and gift taxes
Personal tax and nontax receipts	Motor vehicle licenses
Total receipts before refunds	Property taxes
Income taxes	Other taxes
Estate and gift taxes	Nontaxes
Nontaxes	Corporate profits tax accruals
Less: Tax refunds	Indirect business tax and nontax accruals
Corporate profits tax accruals	Sales tax
Indirect business tax and nontax accruals	State
Total accruals before refunds	General
Excise taxes	Gasoline
Liquor	Liquor
Tobacco	Tobacco
Other	Local
Customs duties	Motor vehicle licenses
Nontaxes	Property taxes
Less: Tax refunds	Other taxes
Contributions for social insurance	Nontaxes
State and local government receipts	Contributions for social insurance
Personal tax and nontax receipts	Federal grants-in-aid
Income taxes	

goods and services, payment of employees, subsidies, etc.; and a third classification of the purpose or function of outlays.

The breakdown of government receipts by type is essential for integrating the government budget with the national income accounts. The United States provides this kind of detail for federal, state, and local governments, as shown in Table 6. As currently presented, the revised UN system does not provide the same kind of detailed information on government receipts. The proposed classifications are shown below.

> Operating surplus
> Withdrawals from entrepreneurial income of quasi-corporate government enterprises
> Property income
>   Interest
>   Dividends
>   Rent
> Casualty insurance claims

Indirect taxes
   Import duties
   Other indirect taxes
Social security contributions
Other direct taxes on income
Compulsory fees, fines and penalties
Current transfers, n.e.c., from the rest of the world
Current transfers, n.e.c., from residents

Although the types of taxes levied by different countries differ substantially, it does appear that the UN classification system places far too much emphasis on the nontax aspects of government receipts, and far too little on the nature of taxes.

With respect to expenditures, the primary difference between the US and the new UN systems is that the US does not recognize either capital formation or capital transactions by the government. The major categories of government expenditure used in the US accounts are given below.

Purchases of goods and services
Transfer payments and net interest paid
Grants-in-aid to state and local government
Subsidies less current surplus of government enterprises

In contrast, the UN shows the following classifications.

Consumption expenditure
Subsidies and other noncontractual transfers
Gross capital formation
Capital transfers
Loans made, net acquisitions of bonds and corporate equity securities, and net addition to investment of quasi-corporate government enterprises

In considering these alternatives, it should be borne in mind that these classifications are normally used in conjunction with information on the expenditures by government on specific programs and purposes. While cross-classifications do become cumbersome, information for the government sector should be produced as part of its normal budgeting and bookkeeping practices; such information is required to assess the nature and impact of specific government programs upon the economy. In light of this, these classifications need to be expanded to provide more information on the exact types of expenditures made. For example, a further separation into purchases from enterprises and compensation of government employees would be useful in showing the degree to

TABLE 7

The US System: Government Expenditures Categories

National defense
  Military services and foreign military assistance
  Atomic energy development
  Other
Space research and technology
General government
  General administration
  General property and records management
  Central personnel management and employment costs
  Net interest paid
  Other
International affairs and finance
  Conduct of foreign affairs and informational activities
  Foreign economic assistance and other transfers
Education
  Elementary and secondary
  Higher
  Other
Health, labor, and welfare
  Health and hospitals
  Sanitation
  Social security and special welfare services
    Public assistance and relief
    Unemployment benefits
    Old age and retirement benefits
    Other
  Civilian safety
    Police
    Fire
    Correction

Labor
Veterans benefits and services
  Education, training, and other benefits
  Disability and pension allowances
  Insurance
  Hospitals and medical care
  Administration and other services
Commerce, transportation, and other services
  Regulation of commerce and finance
  Transportation
    Highways
    Water
    Air
  Housing and community development
    Urban renewal and community facilities
    Public housing
  Public utilities
    Transit
    Electricity
    Water and gas
  Postal services
  Other
Agriculture and agricultural resources
  Stabilization of farm prices and income
  Financing farm ownership and utilities
  Conservation of natural resources
  Other services
Natural resources
  Conservation and development of resources
  Recreation

which the various programs are carried out by the government or are contracted for outside of the government sector. Similarly, it would be useful to distinguish between subsidies to enterprises, transfer payments to individuals, and intergovernmental transfer payments.

The breakdown of government outlays by program will in large part depend upon the organization and legal structure of the government, as well as the functional nature of the programs themselves. It will, of course, be useful in such a presentation to highlight public programs that are of major political or public interest. The present breakdown of government expenditures by type of function for the US is shown in Table 7. Although this breakdown seems quite suitable for the United States, a more general classification system is provided by the UN, as shown in Table 8.

TABLE 8

The UN System: Classification of the Purposes of General Government

1. General government services
   1.1 General administration
   1.2 External affairs
   1.3 Public order and safety
   1.4 General research
2. Defense
3. Education
   3.1 General administration, regulation, and research
   3.2 Schools, universities, and other educational facilities
   3.3 Subsidiary services
4. Health
   4.1 General administration, regulation, and research
   4.2 Hospitals and clinics
   4.3 Individual health services
5. Social security and welfare services
   5.1 Social security and assistance
   5.2 Welfare services
6. Housing and community amenities
   6.1 Housing
   6.2 Community development
   6.3 Sanitary services
7. Other community and social services
   7.1 Recreational and related cultural services
   7.2 Religion and services, n.e.c.
8. Economic services
   8.1 General administration, regulation, and research
   8.2 Agriculture, forestry, fishing, and hunting
   8.3 Mining, manufacturing, and construction
   8.4 Electricity, gas, steam, and water
   8.5 Roads
   8.6 Inland and coastal waterways
9. Other purposes
   9.1 Public-debt transactions
   9.2 Transfers of a general character to other government organs
   9.3 Outlays in connection with disasters and other calamities
   9.4 Outlays, n.e.c.

6 A PROPOSED SYSTEM OF NATIONAL INCOME AND PRODUCT ACCOUNTS

The previous chapters lay the basis for constructing an integrated national economic accounting system. This task is essentially one of fitting the pieces together so that the criteria developed in the discussion can be met. The first step will be to design a system of national income accounts that can serve the same functions as the present US and UN systems, yet also meet many of the objectives of the proposed revision of the UN accounts. These accounts must serve as the nucleus around which other kinds of economic accounting can be developed. At the same time some of the major economic constructs in the national accounts must be substantially altered to make them more comprehensive and more meaningful. Although the proposed revision will be designed primarily to meet the needs of the United States and other similar industrial countries, many of the basic criteria will be equally valid and applicable for less developed countries; in particular, the distinctions between market and nonmarket transactions and the concept of development expenditures will be useful in both the highly developed and less developed countries.

The proposed design of the national income accounts will be illustrated by estimates for the United States for the year 1966. Much of the information required is already available in the present US system. In some cases, however, supplementary information is needed. In these instances, rough estimates of the general magnitudes involved (rounded to the nearest billion) will be shown in the accounts. These estimates are in general conformity with those provided by Kendrick [23].

The proposed accounting structure is that suggested in Chapter 2.

A consolidated income and product account is constructed for the nation as a whole, and income and outlay accounts are provided for each of the three sectors of the economy: enterprises, government, and households. A consolidated external transactions account for the economy completes the system. The list of accounts in the proposed national income accounting system follows.

1. National Income and Product Account
2. Enterprise Sector Accounts
   a. Income and Outlay
   b. Capital Formation
3. Government Sector Accounts
   a. Income and Outlay
   b. Capital Formation
4. Household Sector Accounts
   a. Income and Outlay
   b. Capital Formation
5. External Transactions Account

The full set of these accounts is presented in Appendix C.

The National Income and Product Account

This account is designed to show how the different sectors of the economy are related to the major aggregates of income and product. In concept, this account corresponds quite closely to the national income and product account of the US system and to the domestic product and expenditure account in the revised UN system. It is shown in summary form in Table 9, and in greater detail in Appendix Table C-1.

Although the proposed national income and product account is similar to the US account, there are a number of important differences. On the income side of the account, the primary classification is in terms of income originating in the different sectors of the economy. On the product side of the account, two major components, consumption and gross capital formation, are shown. National income, gross national product at factor cost, gross domestic product at market prices, and gross national product at market prices are all shown explicitly. Sector detail is provided within each major economic construct. Since these constructs have been redefined, however, there is a substantial statistical difference between the data shown in Table 9 and the data provided by the official US national income accounts.

TABLE 9

The Proposed System: National Income and Product Account for the
United States, 1966

(billions of dollars)

Income Originating in:		Consumption	590.0
Enterprises	529.0	Households	435.7
Government	92.6	Government	125.1
Households	38.4	Enterprises	29.2
NATIONAL INCOME	660.0	Gross Capital Formation	308.2
		Households	100.2
Capital Consumption	165.5	Government	81.2
Enterprises	71.6	Enterprises	126.8
Government	36.0	Net Exports	.9
Households	57.9	Exports	37.3
GROSS NATIONAL		Minus: Imports	36.4
PRODUCT AT		GROSS DOMESTIC	
FACTOR COST	825.5	PRODUCT AT MARKET	
		PRICES	899.1
Business consumption and		Net Factor Income From	
transfers	20.7	Abroad	4.2
Indirect taxes	65.1	Factor income from abroad	5.7
Minus: Subsidies	5.4	Minus: Factor income sent	
Statistical discrepancy	−2.6	abroad	1.5
GROSS NATIONAL		GROSS NATIONAL	
PRODUCT AT MARKET		PRODUCT AT MARKET	
PRICES	903.3	PRICES	903.3

The Measurement of Output

Gross national product at market prices as shown in Table 9 exceeds the published figure by $160 billion. This represents a difference of more than 20 per cent. The primary reason for the difference is that the contribution to total output of the stock of durables and past development outlays for both households and government has been included. Second, it has been recognized that businesses customarily write off as current expense both development outlays intended as investment and consumption goods provided free to the public. The reconciliation between the published gross national product for 1966 and the revised figures (in billions of dollars) is shown at the top of page 97.

National income is also influenced by the inclusion of the flow

GROSS NATIONAL PRODUCT, OBE   743.3
   Plus: Services of Durables and Past Development Outlays 116.0
      Households   64.0
      Government   52.0
   Plus: Business Outlays Expensed   44.0
      Development   26.0
      Consumption   18.0
   Total Added to Gross National Product   160.0

GROSS NATIONAL PRODUCT, REVISED   903.3

of services yielded by the stock of durable goods and past development
outlays by households and government. However, since capital consumption is not a part of national income, the difference between the
published national income figures and the revised figure shown in Table 9
is smaller than the difference in gross national product. The increase
in national income is estimated at $43 billion for 1966, or approximately
12 per cent. The net income from durables and past development outlays
accounted for $30 billion of this difference. The adjustment of profits
to reflect the fact that the net expenditures on research and development
are capital outlays rather than current costs increased income originating
in enterprises by $10 billion more. Finally, it should also be recognized
that the surplus of government enterprises, like profits of other enterprises, is a part of the income originating in the enterprise sector. This
added the remaining $3.3 billion. The reconciliation for 1966 is shown
below, in billions of dollars.

NATIONAL INCOME, OBE   616.7
   Plus: Net Income From Durables and Past Development
   Outlays   30.0
      Households   14.0
      Government   16.0
   Plus: Net Development Outlays Charged to Current
   Expense   10.0
   Plus: Surplus of Government Enterprises   3.3
   Total Additions to National Income   43.3

NATIONAL INCOME, REVISED   660.0

Consumption

Total consumption is not shown directly in the present national
income and product account of the United States. However, personal
consumption expenditures and government purchases of goods and

services are shown, and together these do constitute an implicit measure of total consumption. For the year 1966, their sum came to approximately $620 billion.

In revising the implicit total consumption concept of the Office of Business Economics, it is first necessary to take out of personal consumption expenditures and government purchases of goods and services those expenditures that in fact represent outlays for development purposes and for durable goods. For the year 1966, these came to about $175 billion, of which $94 billion was by households and $81 billion was by government. In addition, it is necessary to add to consumption the services provided by past outlays on development and on durables. Ideally, the value of these services should be determined on the basis of equivalent rental value. The Office of Business Economics now imputes the value of the services provided by owner-occupied housing by this method. Such an imputation uses the market value of the services, and thus is directly comparable to other valuations of goods and services. Unfortunately, however, market values are not available for the services of many development outlays and durable goods; in these cases it is necessary to build up a valuation based on cost just as is done for the value of goods provided by the government to the public. Thus, the value of the services of durables and development outlays can be estimated as the capital consumption or amortization adjusted to market prices plus an imputed interest charge on the remaining capital value of the asset or development outlay. These two elements combined provide an imputed measure of the cost of providing the services of the past development outlays and durable goods in the current period. For households, this cost for 1966 came to $24 billion, and for government it came to $52 billion.

Finally, it is necessary to add to the total the consumption carried

Personal Consumption Expenditures, OBE	465.9
Government Purchases of Goods and Services, OBE	154.3
IMPLICIT TOTAL CONSUMPTION, OBE	620.2
Minus: Nonconsumption expenditures	175.4
Households	94.2
Government	81.2
Plus: Services of development and durables	116.0
Households	64.0
Government	52.0
Enterprise consumption	29.2
Total Adjustments	−30.2
TOTAL CONSUMPTION, REVISED	590.0

out directly by the enterprise sector. Some of this will merely reflect the fact that the consumption of nonprofit institutions, which was formerly classified as a personal consumption expenditure, has now been excluded from household consumption. In addition, direct business consumption in the form of goods and services provided free to the public (both customers and employees) must be included. For 1966 it is estimated that total enterprise consumption came to approximately $29 billion.

Taking all of these adjustments together, total OBE consumption of $620 billion for 1966 is reduced by approximately $30 billion. These adjustments are shown on the preceding page, in billions of dollars.

Capital Formation

The Office of Business Economics does not attempt to show total capital formation, but rather presents data only for gross private domestic investment. In order to arrive at a total domestic capital formation estimate, it is necessary to add the durable goods purchased by households and government and the development outlays made by all sectors.

Approximately $70 billion of household durables were purchased in 1966, in addition to the $17 billion of owner-occupied housing already included in gross private domestic investment. For government, it is estimated that somewhat over $40 billion of expenditure was made on durable goods, including structures, construction of highways, and other durables, but excluding military hardware and construction. If owner-occupied housing of $17.2 billion is included as a household rather than an enterprise expenditure, the durable goods expenditures of households and government together would amount to $130 billion, in contrast to $100 billion by enterprises.

Development expenditures are considerably more difficult to define than expenditures on durable goods. To be classified as developmental, the value of the services provided by the expenditure must accrue in future periods rather than entirely in the present period. For the government, this suggests that expenditures on space research and technology, education and training, research in health, and improvement of health facilities can all legitimately be considered developmental. Examination of federal, state, and local expenditures on goods and services for 1966 suggests that approximately $40 billion was spent in these areas. For enterprises, development expenditures are made both as a part of research and development programs and on training and education of employees. It is estimated that these came to approximately $26 billion for 1966. Finally, households contribute to development when they spend their resources on education or on measures for the prevention of sickness such as inoculations. It is estimated that these came to approximately $13 billion in 1966.

As a consequence of these expenditures on durables and development, the total additions to capital formation came to $190 billion, thus making total domestic capital formation $308 billion, in contrast with the OBE estimate of $118 billion for gross private domestic investment. The total flows are shown below, in billions of dollars, for 1966.

GROSS PRIVATE DOMESTIC INVESTMENT, OBE	118.0
Plus: Durables	111.5
Households	70.3
Government	41.2
Plus: Development	78.7
Government	40.0
Enterprises	26.0
Households	12.7
Total Additions	190.2
TOTAL DOMESTIC CAPITAL FORMATION	308.2

Income Originating

On the allocation side of the national income and product account, income originating is shown for the different sectors of the economy: enterprises, government, and households. Within each of these sectors, the account shows how the different factors of production share in the income originating within the sector.

For the enterprise sector, factor shares can be estimated on the basis of the production accounts of establishments engaged in productive activity. In order to explain the measurement of income originating and the derivation of the factor shares for the enterprise sector, it will be useful to examine a hypothetical production account for an individual establishment in the enterprise sector. Such an account is given on the next page. The right-hand side of this account shows the value of product created by this establishment as being composed of sales and the net change in inventories. On the left-hand side, the purchases of goods and services from other producers are shown as intermediate goods and services, and value added or gross product is defined as the total value of product minus the contribution of these intermediate goods and

Compensation of employees	32	Sales	95
Imputed self-employed compensation	3	Change in Inventories	5
Imputed interest on plant and equipment	5		
Net operating surplus (+) or deficit (−)	+17		
Income Originating	57		
Capital consumption	10		
Indirect taxes	8		
Gross Product (value added)	75		
Intermediate Goods and Services	25		
Value of Product	100	Value of Product	100

services. After deducting an allowance for capital consumption (including both depreciation of durables and amortization of past development outlays) and indirect taxes paid to the government, a measure of the net income originating in the establishment is obtained.

The total income originating in the enterprise sector reflects this measurement for all establishments that sell products on the market. The shares of the factors of production are shown in terms of (a) the compensation of employees, (b) self-employed compensation, and (c) imputed interest on the capital (plant and equipment including past development outlays) used by the establishment. When an establishment rents its plant and equipment, the rental payment would of course be included as part of the intermediate goods and services purchased from other producing units, so that neither capital consumption nor imputed interest would be recorded for such equipment in this establishment. In the example shown, the compensation of employees plus the imputed self-employment compensation and the imputed interest do not fully absorb all the income originating, so that a net operating surplus remains. In the case of some nonprofit institutions where the sale of products on the market does not fully reflect their output, it may be necessary to measure income originating from the allocation side of the account, i.e., to add the compensation of employees and the imputed interest on plant, equipment, and past development outlays to arrive at total income originating. This is the same procedure as is followed in estimating the production of general government.

For the enterprise sector as a whole, income originating in 1966 was $529 billion. Of this, $359 billion was paid as compensation to employees. In addition, the number of self-employed proprietors was such that if their services were valued at what they could earn as wage and salary employees in the same industry, or conversely if the cost of replacing their services by paid employees were estimated, another $40 billion would have been needed. It should be emphasized that this figure does not reflect a careful estimate, but is merely based on the number of self-employed in the various industries and the compensation of employees in these industries.

Finally, an estimate of the imputed interest on plant and equipment must also be made to take into account the use of capital by the different establishments. To make this estimate, it is necessary to know the total market value of such plant and equipment used by producing establishments. However, this information is also required if capital consumption is to be estimated correctly. In the case of capital consumption, furthermore, it is also necessary to know the expected future life of the plant and equipment. To impute interest, all that is needed is the present market value of plant and equipment. If the principle of valuing imputations in terms of opportunity costs is followed, and if the element of risk is relegated to surplus rather than included as a payment to capital, there is a strong argument for using the same interest rate to impute the interest charge on plant and equipment for all establishments in all industries in the economy. Such an imputed interest charge would therefore reflect the pure payment to capital as a factor share, and would leave such elements as the imperfection of capital markets, uncertainty, monopoly, etc., to the residual operating surplus or deficit. From the standpoint of the establishment itself, furthermore, this approach is much more meaningful, since the individual productive unit does not pay interest. The interest paid on plant and equipment will be determined largely by the financial structure of the firm owning the establishment, rather than anything inherent in the establishment itself. This role of the firm relative to the establishment will be considered in some detail in the discussion of the enterprise income and outlay account. The factor share breakdown for enterprises from the establishment viewpoint is shown below, in billions of dollars.

Income Originating in Enterprises	529.1
Employee compensation	359.1
Self-employed compensation	40.0
Imputed interest on plant and equipment and	
past development outlays	50.0
Net operating surplus	79.9

In the government sector, income originating is considered to arise from the contribution of the factors of production, rather than from the sale of goods and services on the market. As a consequence, the compensation of government employees, representing the contribution of labor, and the imputed income from durables and development, representing the contribution of capital, constitute the income originating in the government.

Income Originating in General Government	92.6
Employee compensation	76.6
Imputed income from development and durables	16.0

Production originating in the household sector consists of two components: nonmarket production of goods and services directly consumed by households, and net imputed income resulting from past outlays by households on development and durable goods. In the United States, nonmarket production of commodities is rather small. The Office of Business Economics estimates that approximately $1 billion of food was produced and consumed on farms in the year 1966. In less developed countries, this type of subsistence production might be very large, and other productive activities such as making cloth or shoes might constitute additional commodity output of the household. The problem of household production of services is considerably more complex. As Kendrick has noted [23], housewives' services, volunteer labor, and even students' school work constitute important productive activities. In the present system of accounts, however, no estimate is included for these activities. In a similar manner, do-it-yourself projects have been omitted, since it is difficult to distinguish whether these are recreation, or whether they are in fact direct substitutes for market commodities. Imputed income from past expenditures on development and durables is based upon imputing an interest return to the market value of the stock of household durables and the unamortized portion of past development outlays. The results of these imputations are shown below, in billions of dollars.

INCOME ORIGINATING IN THE HOUSEHOLD SECTOR, OBE	38.4
Nonmarket Production	.9
Imputed Income From Development and Durables	37.5
Net imputed housing rent	11.0
Imputed interest on housing	12.5
Imputed interest on other durables and development	14.0

Capital Consumption

Capital consumption consists of two major elements: depreciation on durable goods, and amortization of past development outlays. Depreciation on durable goods for enterprises is the same as that shown in the OBE estimate for capital consumption allowances except that the depreciation of owner-occupied housing has been transferred to the household sector. For general government and for households, depreciation on structures and other durables is based on average length of life. With respect to amortization of development outlays, the amount shown represents a rather arbitrary allocation of development outlays over future periods. The composition of capital consumption is shown below, in billions of dollars.

CAPITAL CONSUMPTION	165.5
Depreciation	122.5
Enterprises	55.6
Government	16.0
Households	50.9
Amortization	43.0
Enterprises	16.0
Government	20.0
Households	7.0

Adjustments

The adjustments to gross national product at factor cost to bring it up to gross national product at market prices consist of (1) business consumption and transfers, (2) indirect taxes less subsidies, and (3) the statistical discrepancy. Business consumption and transfers consist of those outlays that business considers current expenses but that at the same time provide a flow of consumption goods to the economy that represents a net addition to the goods business sells to the public. Indirect taxes again represent a difference between the factor payments that are made and the selling prices of the products, and so must be added to arrive at market prices. Subsidies, on the other hand, need to be subtracted since they represent funds that are provided to business and thus are included in factor payments but that do not arise from goods sold at market prices. Finally, because the two sides of the accounts are estimated from different sources of data there will be a statistical discrepancy. The amounts of various adjustments are shown on the following page, in billions of dollars.

Business Consumption and Transfers	20.7
Indirect Taxes Less Subsidies	59.7
Indirect taxes	65.1
Minus: Subsidies	5.4
Statistical Discrepancy	−2.6

Enterprise Sector Accounts

The enterprise sector has been defined as covering the market economy. Its role in the process of production has already been discussed with respect to the national income and product account in terms of income originating in establishments producing goods and services. Production, however, is only a part of the enterprise activity. The income that originates in establishments flows into various types of firms, such as corporations, proprietorships, government enterprises, and nonprofit institutions. These organizations in turn pay money out to individuals, pay taxes, provide enterprise consumption, and retain funds. They also purchase capital goods, which they finance out of their capital consumption allowances, their saving, and their borrowing. The purpose of the enterprise accounts is to record these activities.

Income and Outlay

This account shows the receipts of enterprises on the right-hand side and the disbursements and income retained by enterprises on the left-hand side. It is shown in Table 10, and in more detail in Appendix Table C-2a. Total enterprise income in this account is identical to the income originating in enterprises shown in the production account. However, enterprises do receive funds in addition to the income that they generate. Households make transfers to nonprofit institutions in the form of gifts (e.g., religious contributions). Interest paid by consumers and by government is also considered to be transfer payments in the national income accounts, rather than income that originates in the enterprise sector. Finally, businesses charge off gifts and consumption expenditures as current expenses, so that these amounts are excluded from enterprise income. From the standpoint of the national income accounts, however, since the outlays are considered to be disbursements by enterprises such funds must be included as receipts.

The form used for income originating in enterprises in the enterprise income and outlay account is quite different from that in the national income and product account. In the latter, productive activity

TABLE 10

The Proposed System: Enterprise Income and Outlay Account for the
United States, 1966

(billions of dollars)

Enterprise Consumption	29.2	Enterprise Income	529.0
		Corporate	360.4
Payments to Households	489.3	Employee compensation	275.9
Employee compensation	359.1	Net interest paid	−2.4
Interest income	40.9	Corporate profits	86.8
Dividends	20.5	Imputed interest on net as-	
Proprietor income	68.8	sets	40.0
		Corporate net profits	46.8
Direct Taxes and Other Pay-			
ments to Government	41.8	Proprietorships	139.2
Corporate profits tax	34.5	Employee compensation	59.2
Surplus of government enter-		Net interest paid	11.2
prises	3.3	Proprietor income	68.8
Interest paid to government	4.0	Imputed self-employed com-	
		pensation	40.0
Retained Income	35.2	Imputed interest on net as-	
Undistributed corporate profits	34.1	sets	15.0
Retained nonprofit income	1.0	Proprietor net profit	13.8
		Government enterprises	11.3
		Employee compensation	8.0
		Surplus	3.3
		Nonprofit institutions	14.0
		Employee compensation	16.0
		Net interest paid	−2.0
		Rest of the world	4.2
		Corporate profits	3.3
		Net interest paid	.9
		Transfers to Nonprofit Insti-	
		tutions From Households	6.5
		Business Consumption and	
		Transfers Expensed	20.7
		Interest Paid by Consumers	25.3
		Interest Paid by Government	13.9
DISBURSEMENTS AND			
RETAINED INCOME OF		RECEIPTS OF	
ENTERPRISES	595.4	ENTERPRISES	595.4

was in terms of establishments, whereas the enterprise income and outlay account considers enterprises in terms of firms or companies. In some instances an establishment and a firm may be the same, but often a single firm owns many establishments, and in addition indulges in financial transactions that affect its operations. A hypothetical example of how income originating in its establishments relates to the operation of a firm is shown below.

Allocations		*Sources*	
Business consumption	50	Income originating in establish-	
Compensation of employees	500	ments	950
Self-employed compensation	50	Business consumption charged to	
Net interest paid	−10	current expense	50
Interest paid	30		
Minus: Interest received	40		
Operating Profit	410		
Imputed interest on net			
assets	300		
Net Profit	110		
TOTAL ALLOCATIONS	1,000	TOTAL SOURCES	1,000

The derivation of the interest factor share at the establishment level differs somewhat from its derivation at the enterprise level. If a firm borrows its capital, the interest it must pay for its use will be a business expense, and the firm's profit is the amount that remains after all business expenses have been paid. In the example shown above, the firm receives more interest than it pays, thus reflecting the fact that the financial assets it owns yield more interest than is required for its financial liabilities, so that its financial assets provide a net contribution to profit. In this hypothetical example, therefore, operating profit of the firm exceeds the operating surplus generated by the establishments owned by the firm. If net interest paid were positive, this would indicate that interest payments on the firm's liabilities exceeded interest receipts on its financial assets so that in fact it was borrowing part of its capital, and net operating profit would be smaller than the operating surplus originating in its establishments. Thus, what the firm's operating profit includes is the contribution of the net assets owned by the firm. If a firm had no financial assets or liabilities, net assets would be equal to plant and equipment, and the imputed interest on net assets would coincide with the imputed interest on plant and equipment for the establishments owned by the enterprise. If a firm borrows heavily, its equity may be considerably less than the value of its plant and equipment, and in this case the imputed interest on its net assets would be considerably lower than that computed for the firm's establishments. Net profit is defined as operating profit minus imputed interest on net assets, and as in the case of the operating surplus it represents a residual over and above the actual and imputed payments to the factors of production.

In computing corporate net profits by this process, it is first necessary to adjust corporate profits for development outlays that are charged as current expense and for amortization of past development outlays, as well as the adjustment for inventory valuation that is normally made. These adjustments, together with the imputed interest on net corporate assets, are shown below, in billions of dollars.

DOMESTIC CORPORATE PROFITS (BOOK VALUE), OBE	80.4
Plus: Inventory valuation adjustment	−1.6
DOMESTIC CORPORATE PROFITS, OBE ADJUSTED	78.8
Plus: Development outlays charged as current expense	20.0
Minus: Amortization of past development outlays	12.0
Total Adjustments to Corporate Profits	8.0
Adjusted Corporate Profits	86.8
Minus: Imputed interest on corporate net assets	40.0
CORPORATE NET PROFITS	46.8

The calculation of imputed interest on net corporate assets is not too difficult. Reliable balance sheet information for the corporate sector is increasingly available, and as in the case of the interest imputation on the national income and product account the interest rate used for the imputation should be constant throughout the economy.

For proprietor and rental income the same principles apply, but the actual adjustments are somewhat more complex. These are shown on the following page, in billions of dollars. In addition to the adjustments shown for corporate enterprises, proprietor and rental income must be adjusted to reflect the fact that imputed rent on owner-occupied housing and nonmarket production do not arise in the enterprise sector, but rather are to be included as output in the household sector. The imputation of self-employed compensation is identical to that which appears for establishments on the national income and product account. As a consequence of all of these adjustments, proprietor net profit is reduced substantially.

PROPRIETOR AND RENTAL INCOME, OBE	79.1
Minus: Inventory valuation adjustment	0.4
PROPRIETOR AND RENTAL INCOME, OBE	
ADJUSTED	78.7
Plus: Development outlays charged as current expense	6.0
Minus: Amortization of past development outlays	4.0
Imputed income on owner-occupied housing	11.0
Nonmarket production	0.9
Total Adjustments to Proprietor and Rental Income	−9.9
PROPRIETOR INCOME, ADJUSTED	68.8
Minus: Self-employed compensation	40.0
Imputed interest on proprietor net assets	15.0
PROPRIETOR NET PROFIT	13.8

The treatment of interest in the proprietor sector is shown below, in billions of dollars.

TOTAL NET INTEREST PAID BY	
BUSINESS, OBE	20.2
Minus: Corporate	−2.4
Nonprofit institutions	−2.0
Rest of world	0.9
Imputed housing	12.5
Total Adjustments	9.0
PROPRIETOR NET INTEREST PAID	11.2

In determining the interest paid to households, similar adjustments must be made. These are shown below, in billions of dollars.

TOTAL NET INTEREST PAID BY BUSINESS,	
OBE	20.2
Plus: Interest paid by government	13.9
Interest paid by households	25.3
Minus: Imputed housing interest	12.5
Interest received by nonprofit institutions	2.0
Interest received by government	4.0
Total Adjustments	20.7
PERSONAL INTEREST INCOME, ADJUSTED	40.9

It should be noted that the imputed interest appearing in the national income and product account for enterprises as a whole on an establishment basis differs conceptually and statistically from the total imputed interest appearing in the enterprise income and outlay account. If the equity of firms exactly equalled the amount of their plant, equipment, and past development outlays, the imputed interest for establishments and for firms would be equal. However, if firms own additional financial assets in the form of government securities or consumer debt, the imputed interest of firms in the enterprise income and outlay account will exceed the imputed interest of establishments in the income and product account. Imputed interest both for establishments and for firms should show how much of the return normally considered operating surplus or profit is in fact a return on plant and equipment or net assets.

It should also be noted that the imputation of interest that is carried out to obtain a net operating surplus or profit concept is of an entirely different character from the imputation of interest for banking services. This latter imputation is still made in the accounts, representing an imputed transaction between sectors and included in the interest paid by the enterprise sector to households. For the year 1966, it amounted to almost $9 billion.

Because nonprofit institutions are removed from the household sector and treated as enterprises, it is necessary to show explicitly the transfers that households make to nonprofit institutions. On the basis of information contained in the present national income accounts, the amount of employee compensation paid by nonprofit institutions is estimated at $16 billion, and the net interest they receive at approximately $2.0 billion. In addition, it is estimated that households provide about $6.5 billion in gifts such as religious and charitable contributions.

The consumption of nonprofit institutions and of businesses providing services such as radio, television, support of newspapers, subsidized cafeterias, and travel expenses is estimated at approximately $29 billion for the year 1966, as shown below, in billions of dollars.

ENTERPRISE CONSUMPTION	29.2
Business Consumption	18.7
Mass media support	13.0
Provision of consumption goods	5.7
Nonprofit Consumption	10.5
Religious	5.0
Health, education, welfare	3.5
Other	2.0

These are rough estimates, and probably quite conservative. The extent of business consumption expenditures could be determined by more detailed examination of a sample of enterprise accounts, together with tax information.

Finally, it should be noted that the enterprise income and outlay account includes the surplus of government enterprises, both as a part of income originating and as a payment to government. In the US accounts, the surplus of government enterprises is combined with subsidies, and thus netted out of both income originating and income received by government. The data shown in the accounts refer to state and local enterprises only. The surplus of federal government enterprises (if any) is still combined with federal subsidies.

Capital Formation

This account shows the composition of gross enterprise capital formation and the saving, net borrowing, and lending by the enterprise sector. It is shown in Table 11 and Appendix Table C-2b.

Development expenditures by enterprises are made up of two types of expenditures: research and development, and education and training. Fairly reliable information now exists on research and development expenditures by enterprises. Conceptually, however, it is still diffi-

TABLE 11

The Proposed System: Enterprise Capital Formation Account for the
United States, 1966

(billions of dollars)

Development Expenditures	26.0	Enterprise Capital Con-	
Research and development	18.0	sumption	71.6
Education and training	8.0	Depreciation	55.6
		Corporate	39.0
Expenditures on Durables	87.4	Proprietors	15.6
Structures	35.1	Nonprofit institutions	1.0
Other durables	52.3		
		Amortization	16.0
Change in Inventories	13.4	Corporate	12.0
		Proprietors	4.0
Net Foreign Investment	2.2	Retained Income	35.2
		Corporate	34.2
		Nonprofit institutions	1.0
		Net Borrowing From (+) or	
		Net Lending to (−) Other	
		Sectors	+24.9
		Households	+17.7
		Government	+7.2
		Statistical Discrepancy	−2.6
		GROSS SAVING, NET BOR-	
GROSS ENTERPRISE		ROWING, AND LENDING	
CAPITAL FORMATION	129.0	BY ENTERPRISES	129.0

cult to distinguish those expenditures that should be written off as part of current expense and those which are obviously of a long-term nature. With respect to education and training, formal training and education programs certainly should be included, and to some extent on-the-job training can also be considered developmental. It is quite difficult to estimate the magnitude of these training programs, and they may in fact be much larger than the figure shown. With respect to expenditures on durable goods, the construction of owner-occupied housing has been deducted from enterprise expenditures on structures, since owner-occupied housing is considered to be capital formation by households. The remaining items in gross enterprise capital formation are the same as those in the OBE figure for gross private investment.

On the savings side of the account, depreciation of owner-occupied housing has been deducted, and amortization of development expenditures by corporate and noncorporate enterprises has been added. A small amount of retained income has been shown for nonprofit institutions—this is a transfer from the saving of the household sector. Net borrowing by enterprises from other sectors amounted to about $25 billion, of which $18 billion was borrowing from households and $7 billion borrowing from the government sector, i.e., the enterprise sector reduced its net holdings of government assets during this period by approximately $7 billion.

A problem arises of whether the depreciation allowances charged by enterprises for tax purposes do reflect the actual depreciation that is taking place. There are two major sources of bias in this estimate. First, it is to the interest of enterprises to charge off plant and equipment as rapidly as possible in order to reduce taxes. There is considerable evidence that the length of life used by enterprises for tax purposes is considerably shorter than the actual life over which assets are used. This is especially true with structures, where the structure may be of considerable value even after it has been fully written off. The government's interest in stimulating investment has led to the introduction of accelerated depreciation, which results in depreciation allowances that are purposely larger than actual depreciation. For these reasons there is a substantial tendency to overstate depreciation in the current period.

On the other hand, depreciation allowances are tied to allocating the original cost of the asset over future periods. If the prices of capital goods increase over time the depreciation charged will not reflect replacement cost. Businessmen are keenly aware of this, and have often urged that replacement cost depreciation be allowed for tax purposes. From an economic standpoint there is some justification for such a valuation of depreciation, although from a tax standpoint it would result in an element of capital gain going untaxed. In any event, it is obvious that the use of original cost rather than replacement value does tend to exert a downward bias on depreciation allowances.

Thus, depreciation allowances are subject to both an upward bias through the acceleration of depreciation allowances and a downward bias through the use of original cost instead of replacement value. Some estimates of the magnitude of these biases are available. In a study done by Helen Stone Tice [29], replacement cost depreciation on the stock of private structures and producer durables was estimated for the period 1900–62. A 1959 depreciation survey by the Treasury Department indicated that the lives actually being used for tax purposes were 20 per cent shorter than the Treasury Department's Bulletin F lives [30]. In computing depreciation, Mrs. Tice used the service lives indicated in Bulletin F and adjusted the value of the capital stock to replacement cost. The net result of this lengthening of service life and adjustment to replacement value, however, was not significant. Mrs. Tice obtained a total estimated depreciation allowance of $49.1 billion for 1962, in contrast with the figure of $50.0 billion reported in the national income accounts. In other words, the two biases tended to offset each other. For individual industries or sectors, however, larger discrepancies might appear.

Government Sector Accounts

The government sector has the same definition in the proposed system as in the current US and UN accounts: it embraces general government activities that are not of an enterprise nature. Although the principle is clear, there are often difficulties in determining whether a specific government organization is in fact acting like an enterprise, or whether, even though it receives some fees or sells some products, it is essentially a government agency.

Income and Outlay

This account is quite similar to the present government account, except for the alteration of some flows to recognize that some government expenditures do constitute capital formation, and that income is

TABLE 12

The Proposed System: Government Income and Outlay Account for the
United States, 1966

(billions of dollars)

Consumption	125.1	Indirect Taxes	65.1
Current expenditures	73.1		
Imputed services of develop-		Direct Taxes and Other Pay-	
ment and durables	52.0	ments by Enterprises	41.8
		Corporate profits tax	34.5
Subsidies	5.4	Surplus of government	
		enterprises	3.3
Transfers to Households	41.2	Interest paid to government	4.0
		Tax Payments by Households	113.4
Transfers to Abroad	2.3		
		Transfers From Abroad	*
Current Surplus	48.4		
		Imputed Income From De-	
		velopment and Durables	16.0
		Minus: Government Interest	
		Paid	13.9
GOVERNMENT CUR-			
RENT OUTLAYS AND		GOVERNMENT	
SURPLUS	222.4	RECEIPTS	222.4

NOTE: An asterisk denotes less than 0.05.

received from the services of past development outlays and durables.
The government income and outlay is shown in Table 12 and Appendix
Table C-3a.

Government receipts have been increased by three items. First, the
surplus of government enterprises is treated as a receipt instead of being
netted against subsidies. In the United States this is important since the
government enterprises that yield surpluses are mainly those operated
at the state and local levels (e.g., publicly owned utilities), and those
receiving subsidies represent different types of activities. Certain government enterprises are purposely run at a deficit as part of their function,
for instance subway systems or the Commodity Credit Corporation. In
such cases, it might be useful to distinguish these intended deficits and
treat them as subsidies, but also to recognize that the deficits of other
government enterprises are often no more intentional than those of other
nonprofit enterprises. Second, the interest received by the government

is shown as part of the income of the government, rather than netted against interest paid by the government. Finally, the net imputed income that the government receives from past development and durables expenditures minus the interest the government pays should be shown explicitly, and included as part of total receipts. These adjustments are shown below, in billions of dollars.

Government Receipts, OBE	213.0
Plus: Current surplus of government enterprises	3.3
Interest received by government	4.0
Net imputed income	2.1
Total Adjustments	9.4
Government Receipts, Revised	222.4

With respect to government expenditures, those outlays of the government that have their primary impact in future periods should be excluded from current consumption, and the services provided by past development outlays and durables owned by the government should be added to arrive at a total consumption figure. These adjustments are shown below.

GOVERNMENT PURCHASES OF GOODS AND SERVICES, OBE	154.3
Minus: Nonconsumption Expenditures:	81.2
Durables	40.0
Development	41.2
CURRENT CONSUMPTION EXPENDITURES	73.1
Plus: Imputed Services of Development and Durables:	52.0
Imputed interest	16.0
Capital consumption	16.0
Amortization	20.0
GOVERNMENT CONSUMPTION	125.1

Since the government income and outlay account shows government consumption instead of total purchases of goods and services, the surplus in this account becomes $48.4 billion, in contrast with the $3.2 billion surplus in the OBE government receipts and expenditure account.

Capital Formation

This account is shown in Table 13 and Appendix Table C-3b. Development expenditures constitute approximately half of total government gross capital formation in the account. Government expenditures

TABLE 13

The Proposed System: Government Capital Formation Account for the
United States, 1966

(billions of dollars)

Development Expenditures	40.0	Capital Consumption	36.0
Research and development	10.0	Depreciation	16.0
Education	20.0	Amortization	20.0
Health	10.0		
		Current Surplus	48.4
Structures Expenditures	24.2	Net Borrowing From (+) or	
Buildings	8.9	Net Lending to (−) Other	
Highways and streets	8.3	Sectors	−3.2
Other	7.0	Households	4.0
		Enterprises	−7.2
Other Durables Expenditures	17.0	GROSS SAVING AND NET BORROWING OR	
GOVERNMENT GROSS		LENDING BY GOVERN-	
CAPITAL FORMATION	81.2	MENT	81.2

on research and development amounted to approximately $10 billion, expenditures on education to another $20 billion, and health expenditures of a developmental nature accounted for the remaining $10 billion. Structures accounted for approximately $24 billion, of which $9 billion were buildings and $8 billion highways and streets. Finally, it is very roughly estimated that other durable goods expenditures by government exclusive of defense came to approximately $17 billion. There is at present no adequate basis for obtaining an estimate of this element of gross capital formation, but it would be possible to develop such an estimate by analyzing the detailed budget information contained in the accounts of the various types of government.

With respect to capital consumption, major conceptual problems arise in determining the proper rates of depreciation and amortization. It is difficult to determine over what period highways, public parks, and other public facilities should be depreciated, or how research and development and health expenditures should be amortized. Nevertheless, the recognition that such expenditures have their primary benefits in the future rather than the present is a significant improvement, and it would be a more serious error if they were written off all at the time of expenditure. Finally, in 1966 the general government had a net surplus on current and capital account. This is reflected in the net lending to the rest of the economy of $3.2 billion, which is equal to the surplus shown in the OBE government receipts and expenditure account.

Household Sector Accounts

The household sector relates to individuals in their role as households. The activities of nonprofit institutions have been transferred into the enterprise sector. Conversely, owner-occupied housing, which is treated as an imputed enterprise in the US and UN accounts, is here treated as an asset of the household sector that yields imputed income to households.

Income and Outlay

This account for households, shown in Table 14 and Appendix Table C-4a, shows the income and current consumption of households.

TABLE 14

The Proposed System: Household Income and Outlay Account for the
United States, 1966

(billions of dollars)

Tax Payments	113.4	Payments by Enterprises	489.3
		Employee compensation	359.1
Disposable Income	506.8	Interest income	40.9
CONSUMPTION	435.7	Dividends	20.5
Current expenditures	339.4	Proprietor income	68.8
Nonmarket production	.9		
Imputed services of development and durables	95.4	Compensation of Government Employees	76.6
Transfers to Nonprofit Institutions	6.5	Transfers From Government	41.2
Transfers to Abroad	.6	Transfers From Abroad	*
Current Saving	64.0	Income Originating in Households	38.4
		Nonmarket production	.9
		Imputed income of development and durables	37.5
		Minus: Consumer Interest Paid	25.3
PERSONAL CURRENT OUTLAY AND SAVING	620.2	PERSONAL INCOME	620.2

NOTE: An asterisk denotes less than 0.05.

Personal income is considerably larger than the personal income shown by the Office of Business Economics. Two major elements, social security contributions and net imputed interest on household durables, account for most of the difference. The OBE does not include social security contributions as a part of personal income, but since they are in fact withheld by employers in precisely the same way as are personal income taxes there seems little reason on economic grounds to differentiate between social security contributions and other personal taxes. Adjustments to personal income include the adjustment for interest and dividends paid to nonprofit institutions and the adjustments already discussed with respect to proprietors' income, which becomes income of the household. Finally, business transfers are now excluded from personal income on the ground that they are either business gifts to nonprofit institutions or consumer bad debts, both of which are now treated as giving rise to enterprise consumption. These adjustments are shown below, in billions of dollars.

PERSONAL INCOME, OBE	584.0
Plus: Social security contributions	38.2
Net imputed interest on durables	13.1
Total Additions	51.3
Minus: Adjustments to:	
Interest	1.5
Dividends	1.0
Proprietor income	9.9
Business transfers	2.7
Total Adjustments	−15.1
PERSONAL INCOME, ADJUSTED	620.2

For personal consumption expenditures, another set of adjustments is required to remove the expenditures by households on development and durables, the expenditures by nonprofit institutions and businesses (business transfer payments), and the imputed transactions taking place within households. It will also be necessary to add the nonmarket production and the imputed services provided by household durables and development expenditures. This reconciliation is shown on the following page, in billions of dollars.

Since the consumption of nonprofit institutions has been deducted from consumer expenditures, it will be necessary to show explicitly in the household income and outlay account the transfers that households make to nonprofit institutions. In 1966 these were estimated at $6.5

CONSUMER EXPENDITURES, OBE	465.9
Minus: Development expenditures	12.7
Durables	70.3
Nonprofit institutions	70.3
Nonmarket production	.9
Imputed housing income	31.4
Capital consumption	7.9
Imputed interest	12.5
Net rent	11.0
Business transfer payments	2.7
Total Adjustments	126.5
CONSUMPTION EXPENDITURES	339.4
CONSUMPTION OF SERVICES OF STOCK OF DURABLES	
AND PAST DEVELOPMENT OUTLAYS:	96.3
Imputed housing income	31.4
Nonmarket production	.9
Imputed services of household development outlays and durables	64.0
Interest	14.0
Capital consumption	50.0
Automobiles	18.0
Durables	25.0
Development	7.0
HOUSEHOLD CONSUMPTION	435.7

billion. As a result of all of these changes, current saving in the revised account is $64 billion, in contrast with personal saving reported by the OBE of $30 billion.

Capital Formation

Gross capital formation by households for 1966 is estimated at approximately $100 billion. This is shown in Table 15 and Appendix Table C-4b. Approximately $13 billion was spent by households on development expenditures, of which $7 billion was education and $5 billion health. The estimate of $5 billion for health expenditures does not reflect total expenditures by households on medical care; for 1966, this amounted to over $31 billion. The estimate of $5 billion has been inserted purely to indicate that some relatively small fraction of total health expenditures reflect measures of a preventive nature.

With respect to expenditures on durables, approximately $17 billion was spent on owner-occupied houses, $30 billion on automobiles, and $40 billion on other durables. As in the case of the government capital formation account, the estimation of capital consumption is difficult. The figure of approximately $8 billion for depreciation on owner-occupied

TABLE 15

The Proposed System: Household Capital Formation Account for the
United States, 1966

(billions of dollars)

Development Expenditures	12.7	Capital Consumption	57.9
Health	5.0	Depreciation	50.9
Education	6.7	Owner-occupied housing	7.9
Other	1.0	Automobiles	18.0
		Other	25.0
Durables Expenditures	87.5		
Owner-occupied houses	17.2	Amortization	7.0
Automobiles	29.9	Health	3.5
Other	40.4	Education	3.0
		Other	.5
		Current Saving	64.0
		Net Borrowing From (+) or Lending to (−) Other Sectors	−21.7
		Enterprises	−17.7
		Government	− 4.0
GROSS CAPITAL FORMATION BY HOUSEHOLDS	100.2	GROSS SAVING AND NET BORROWING OR LENDING BY HOUSEHOLDS	100.2

housing is the same as that used by OBE, but the depreciation for automobiles and other durables is based on rough service life assumptions. The estimates of amortization are even rougher, but they are intended to show that the amortization of past development expenditures is substantially lower than the current rate of development expenditures, since these categories are growing in importance.

Finally, households are shown as net lenders, in the amount of approximately $22 billion. The holdings of government securities by the household sector increased approximately $4 billion, and their acquisition of other financial assets (aside from revaluation) amounted to $18 billion.

External Account

The external account shown in Table 16 and Appendix Table C-5 is almost completely identical to the foreign transactions account of the

TABLE 16

The Proposed System: External Transactions Account for the United States, 1966

(billions of dollars)

Exports	37.3	Imports	36.4
Factor income from abroad	5.7	Factor income to abroad	1.5
Transfers to households	*	Transfers from households	.6
Transfers to government	*	Transfers from government	2.3
		Net foreign investment	2.2
		PAYMENTS TO ABROAD AND NET FOREIGN	
RECEIPTS FROM ABROAD	43.0	INVESTMENT	43.0

NOTE: An asterisk denotes less than 0.05.

Office of Business Economics. The total of the account is the same, and the only significant difference is that factor income from abroad and factor income sent abroad are shown explicitly rather than as a net balance.

7 THE PROPOSED INTEGRATION OF NATIONAL ECONOMIC ACCOUNTS

The System of Integrating the Economic Accounts

The national income accounts proposed in the previous chapter have been constructed so that they readily deconsolidate into the other forms of economic accounting. This method of integration is currently used by the Office of Business Economics to integrate input-output information, by the Federal Reserve Board to show the relation of flow-of-funds to the national income accounts, and by the new UN system as the basis for its general economic accounting structure.

From a logical viewpoint, one can conceive of any set of economic accounts as being essentially derived from other sets of economic accounts. In the early stages of economic accounting, integration was thought of in terms of a large n-dimensional matrix, and in many ways the new UN accounting system reverts to this idea in its matrix representation. However, the detailed data required for such a multi-dimensional matrix do not make it easy to present in statistical form, or to understand. The opposite procedure—starting with an aggregated system and deriving the detailed systems as different kinds of deconsolidation and more detailed breakdowns—permits the system to develop as required for different kinds of statistical analysis; additional information can be introduced at the detailed level without altering the basic structure of the system. In providing the framework, it is more reasonable to develop an aggregated set of data as a central core and to show detailed information as deconsolidations than to attempt to specify as the basic elements in the system masses of detailed data that can be aggregated in a number of different ways to provide alternative constructs. The coverage of national income accounting is quite comprehensive, and shows how the current activity of the economy is related to past accumulations and how in turn it provides additional accumulation for the future. Deconsolidation of the national income accounts provides considerably greater flexibility in the development of analytic information and permits changes in the specification of the detailed data without affecting the more aggregated economic constructs. The more detailed data, furthermore, never need to be published, but can be kept in machine readable form if the principles underlying its construction can be adequately specified.

An integrated system of national economic accounts based upon the proposed national income accounting system is shown in Figure 5. The four basic types of national income accounts are shown in the blocks across the top of the diagram. The first block (Account 1) shows the national income and product account. The second block (Accounts 2a, 3a, and 4a) shows the income and outlay accounts for enterprises, government, and households. The third block (Accounts 2b, 3b, and 4b) shows the capital formation accounts for enterprises, government, and households. The last block (Account 5) shows the external trans-actions for all sectors. The other forms of economic accounts are shown as deconsolidations or more detailed breakdowns of these accounts.

The input-output table (Account 6) is a deconsolidation of the national income and product account by industry and sector. It provides information on the value of production for each industry and sector in terms of the inputs required from other industries and sectors. The gross product for a specific industry or sector is the value of production minus interindustry purchases. It would be possible to break the input-output account into two pieces as has been done in the new United Nations revision, one showing the commodities produced by industries and sectors, and the other showing commodities consumed by them. For summary presentations, however, casting the data into a single table showing inputs and outputs by industry provides sufficient information.

In addition to current input-output accounts, data on capital formation taking place in the different industries and sectors of the economy are needed. These data (Account 7) can be derived directly from the breakdown of the data provided in the individual sector capital accounts.

An international trade account (Account 8) classifying exports and imports by industrial origin and country provides a related form of industry information. For some countries with large foreign trade sec-

FIGURE 5

The Proposed Integration of the National Economic Accounts

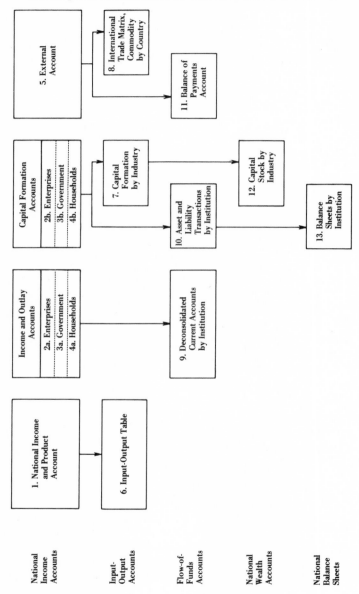

tors, it is important to be able to relate the functioning of the domestic economy to world trade flows. The classifications provided for this type of information should fit in with the industry classifications used for the input-output accounts and for capital formation by industry.

The flow-of-funds accounts provide information on the total sources and uses of funds by institutional sector. They can be thought of as consisting of two major kinds of flows: (1) current income and outlay flows, and (2) asset and liability transactions. The flow-of-funds accounts can be derived as deconsolidations of the sector income and outlay and capital formation accounts. Accounts 9, 10, and 11 in Figure 5 reflect such a deconsolidation, in which the sectoring is expanded to include institutions by legal form of organization, with particular emphasis on the financial sector of the economy. The deconsolidation of the income and outlay accounts should show transactions among the subsectors. The deconsolidation of the sector capital formation accounts is somewhat more elaborate, because what need to be shown are the transactions by specific types of asset and liability for each sector. Any desired level of detail or grossness can be provided by classifying assets and liabilities in terms of types of instrument and sector or subsector issuing the instrument. The balance of payments (Account 11) can also be considered part of the flow-of-funds accounts; it shows the relation of the rest of the world to the domestic economy.

National wealth (Account 12) is a logical extension of Account 7. The national wealth account provides information on total capital stock by type of good for each industry and sector of the economy; it is, of course, directly related to the use of the capital stock by different industries and sectors.

Finally, the national balance sheet (Account 13) represents a cumulation of the transactions in assets and liabilities by institutional sector shown in Account 10. The same classification of institutional sectors and subsectors and the same item classifications of assets and liabilities by type should be used in the balance sheet (Account 13) as were used for transactions in assets and liabilities in Account 10.

This system of integration permits a great deal of flexibility. It is important, however, that consistent classification systems be used throughout the economic accounting system so that the data in one part of the system can be related in analytic terms to data appearing elsewhere. Appendix Tables C-1 through C-13 show how these thirteen accounts can be implemented in terms of sets of interrelated classifications. However, the system of integration does not depend on the adoption of any special classification system; this choice can best be made in terms of analytic needs for the different kinds of information.

The Input-Output Accounts

The input-output accounts include three separate tables: (1) the input-output matrix showing interindustry transactions, (2) an account showing industry and sector capital formation by type of good, and (3) a breakdown of exports and imports in terms of the type of industrial product and country or area of trade.

The Input-Output Table

This table provides interindustry transaction data. It is a direct deconsolidation of the national income and product account. The general form of the input-output matrix is shown below.

	I Intermediate Sales (by industry and sector)	II Final Sales (by sector)	III Value of Sales
I Purchases of Goods and Services (by industry and sector)	X_{11}	X_{12}	X_{13}
II Gross Product Originating (by type of factor cost)	X_{21}	X_{22}	X_{23}
III Value of product	X_{31}	X_{32}	X_{33}

Interindustry transactions are shown in X_{11}. Final sales by industries to sectors are shown in X_{12}. The row total X_{13} is the sum of X_{11} and X_{12} and shows total sales by industry and by sector. Gross product originating in terms of the various elements of factor cost for different industries is shown in X_{21}. There is no data in X_{22}, since by definition all factors of production are employed by the industries and sectors as producing units, and none are purchased directly as part of final sales. The row total X_{23} provides for the total economy exactly the same information that appears on the income side of the consolidated production account. Column total X_{31} is exactly equal to row total X_{13}, industry by industry. The expenditure side of the consolidated production account is shown by sector in column total X_{32}. The corner of the matrix, X_{33}, is equal to the sum of all current income and product transactions.

Conventional input-output tables often do not contain information on the use of the factors of production. The inclusion of such information as an integral part of the table is very useful, however. The suggested breakdown is that developed for the income side of the consolidated production statement, as shown below.

> Gross product originating at factor cost:
> Compensation of employees
> Compensation of self-employed
> Imputed interest on capital
> Net operating surplus
> Capital consumption

The treatment of imports in the input-output table corresponds quite closely to their treatment in the national income and product account. Imports are shown as a negative item in the use of final product. In input-output terms, this means that imports are classified with domestic production of a similar kind; thus, the total uses of a given commodity can exceed domestic production by the amount of imports. It is true that some commodities may not have any corresponding domestic industry. In order to meet this problem, separate industries for those products produced only abroad can be shown as rows in the input-output table.

Appendix Table C-6 gives an example of the arrangement of the stub and column headings for the input-output table. In this table, the industry input-output classifications shown are those used by the United States Department of Commerce. Any other system of industrial classification could be used without altering the general form of the account.

Capital Formation

This is the second set of data derived from the production account classified by input-output industries. Although it would be possible to classify capital goods in terms of industries producing them, such a presentation would have limited usefulness since only a few industries actually do produce products that enter into capital formation. A more useful approach is a commodity classification of capital goods that would indicate the technological differences in the different kinds of capital goods, and at the same time would fit into input-output industry classifications. For example, it would be useful to break construction into residential structures, office buildings, plants, and other facilities. The classification by type of capital good used in the national income accounts is directly pertinent. It would also be useful to show inventories in terms of their stage in the production process, i.e., raw materials, work in process, and finished goods. Finally, capital formation of government and households must be included in order to cover all capital formation done in the economy.

The capital accounts for the various industries and sectors should also show gross saving of each sector arising from capital consumption and net operating surplus or saving. If gross investment by an industry or sector is larger than this gross saving, its capital formation will require a net financial contribution by other industries or sectors. Conversely if a given industry or sector generates gross savings in excess of its gross investment, it will be providing financing to other industries or sectors.

Appendix Table C-7 shows possible stub and column headings for input-output capital accounts. The classification by type of capital good shown is that used in the United States national income accounts.

The International Trade Matrix

This account shows goods and services imported and exported in terms of the input-output industry classification and the countries with which the trade is carried on. Such a table is particularly useful for those less developed countries that depend heavily on international trade for the sale of their domestic production and their supply of industrial products. This part of the system makes it possible to integrate the input-output table into the analysis of world trade. Appendix Table C-8 presents the form for such a table. The net trade balance shown in this table is the difference between exports and imports of goods and services.

The Flow-of-Funds Accounts

These accounts present information for the institutional sectors in terms of (1) a deconsolidation of their current account activities,

(2) their asset and liability transactions, and (3) the balance of payments. Together they are sufficient for the analysis of the flow of funds of the different sectors in relation to the economic activity of the system.

Deconsolidation of the Current Accounts

The process of deconsolidation of the current accounts for enterprises, governments, and households is quite straightforward. The information in the current accounts for each of the major sectors is merely shown for an increased number of subsectors. Although it would be possible to show the full set of to-whom from-whom financial transactions, this is not needed for most analyses.

For the enterprise sector, the subsectors shown should be directly related to the broad institutional sectoring already given in the enterprise current account. Specifically this means that corporate, noncorporate, and government enterprises, and nonprofit institutions should be recognized as major subsectors and these in turn broken down into major industry divisions as shown below.

> Agriculture, forestry, and fisheries
> Mining
> Contract construction
> Manufacturing
>   Durable
>   Nondurable
> Transportation
> Communication
> Electric, gas, and sanitary services
> Wholesale and retail trade
> Finance, insurance, and real estate
> Services

Not all of these industry divisions will be important for all the major subsectors. The industry division classification can be collapsed when appropriate.

For the government, the institutional subsectoring should be in terms of recognized governmental bodies having both taxing and budgetary authority. This suggests that for the current account deconsolidation there should be no breakdown of the federal government, but that individual states and possibly local governments should be shown as subsectors. A breakdown such as in Appendix Table C-9b would be very useful for the study of the behavior and the role of the different levels of government in the economy.

The breakdown of the household sector can be based upon the occupational status of the head of the household. Proprietors, employees, and individuals not in the labor force should be distinguished as separate major subgroups. Proprietors and employees could be further classified by the industrial divisions provided for the enterprise sector, thus showing such groups as farm households, retail trade, professional proprietors, etc. Households not in the labor force could be further broken down to show the retired and institutional population. Such subsectoring would permit the household data to be directly related to the subsectoring of the enterprise sector.

Thus, all the sector current accounts can be deconsolidated as shown in Appendix Tables C-9a, C-9b, and C-9c. The stubs in these tables are closely related to the information provided in the consolidated current account for each major sector.

Asset and Liability Transactions Accounts

These accounts represent a more complex deconsolidation of the capital formation accounts. The basic elements of this deconsolidation are shown below.

Transactions in Assets and Liabilities

	Institutional Sectors
Assets	
Development expenditures	
Durable goods expenditures	
Inventories	
Financial assets	
Liabilities and equities	
Liabilities	
Equities	
Retained income	
Realized capital gains	

Development and durable goods expenditures and inventories are obtained directly from the investment side of the capital formation account, and are broken down by the institutional subsectors already discussed. In the sector capital account, however, the financial transactions involving assets and liabilities are represented only by *net* financial investment.

Deconsolidation involves showing separately the financial transactions affecting the assets and liabilities for each subsector. Finally, equities not only reflect the current saving or surplus of a sector, but also changes in equity caused by sales of assets resulting in capital gains that are not reflected in current income. It will therefore be necessary to include an item for realized capital gains.

It should be emphasized that this treatment of transactions in assets and liabilities does not take into account the revaluation of assets and liabilities except to the extent that these revaluations are realized by *actual* transactions. Much as the national income accounts eliminate changes in the value of existing inventories from the measurement of income, so also unrealized valuation changes in assets are excluded from the account showing transactions in assets and liabilities.

Appendix Table C-10 shows a classification of the transactions in assets and liabilities based on that used by Raymond Goldsmith in his study of national balance sheets [31]. Other systems of asset and liability classification could be used without altering the general form of this account.

For financial analysis, both further subsectoring of the financial sector and more detailed classifications of financial assets and liabilities will be required. Such highly specific information is best developed separately as sets of tables related to the more general table for the economy as a whole. It is not desirable to introduce such a level of detail for all sectors since it would require data that are both difficult to estimate and of little analytical use.

Balance of Payments

This account records the net financial transactions of the rest of the world with the domestic economy. The usefulness of integration of the balance of payments with the national income accounts has been widely recognized.

For present purposes the balance of payments is shown on a net basis as it is presented in the United States national income accounts; it is directly related to the "net trade balance" derived in Appendix Table C-8. Appendix Table C-11 shows the balance of payments in terms of the net trade balance, net payments sent abroad, and the net change in monetary reserves.

National Wealth and Balance Sheets

The national wealth account and the national balance sheet provide information on the stock of durable and development goods and services by industry of use, and on the composition of assets and liabilities and equities by institutional subsector, respectively. Both of these accounts are logical extensions of information already contained in the national economic accounting system.

National Wealth

This account, as shown in Appendix Table C-12, has stub and column headings directly comparable to those in Appendix Table C-7 on capital formation by industry and sector. Conceptually, this account represents the cumulation of capital formation over time. It can be calculated on a perpetual inventory basis, taking into account both capital consumption and revaluation to reflect changes in prices. For economic analysis, it is most useful if this measurement of the capital stock reflects market valuations and reproduction costs. Given the existence of capital formation data for previous periods, it should be possible for those interested in the construction of economic models concerned with the vintage of capital to obtain data on the vintage as well as type of capital for each industry. On the equity side neither capital consumption nor amortization will appear, since this account is drawn up in terms of the market value of assets. Instead, the following three items will appear: (a) cumulative net operating surplus, (b) cumulative net financial balance, and (c) revaluation of assets from original cost minus capital consumption.

The Balance Sheet

This account, as shown in Appendix Table C-13, has stubs and column headings directly comparable to those in Appendix Table C-10, the transactions in assets and liabilities by institutional subsector. Since the balance sheets are in market values of the assets and liabilities, it will be necessary to include an additional item in equity to show the amount of unrealized capital gain resulting from changes in the market value of assets and liabilities held by the different subsectors. As suggested by Gorman [32], it would also be useful to provide a special table showing the revaluations of assets and liabilities for the balance sheet. This would be similar to the current practice of showing the implicit price deflators in the national income accounts.

Related Economic and Social Data

Although the formal economic accounts provide a general framework for economic and social data, they do not, of course, contain all required information, and it is necessary to develop supplementary sets of information that can be directly related to them.

Prices and Real Measurements

One of the first kinds of information the economist wishes to develop outside the formal system of transactions accounts is constant price data. Since the economic transactions reported in the national economic accounts reflect changes in both prices and quantities, the user must adjust these data if he wishes to obtain measures that reflect quantity changes alone. Customarily, constant price data are provided for two different kinds of breakdown: final expenditures and production by industry. The final expenditure breakdown is obtained by using price indexes to deflate transactions in current prices, or by directly obtaining volume measures for specific categories of final expenditures. Generally, constant price data are computed for all categories of consumption, capital formation, imports, and exports, all valued at market prices. For production by industry, it is usually necessary to deflate both the inputs into an industry and the outputs from an industry in order to obtain deflated value added. Again in some cases it may be possible to use volume measures of the output of an industry or of inputs to obtain more accurate measures.

If data on national wealth are available, it may also be desirable to obtain real measures of the capital stock in different periods. Such measurement is necessary if estimates of depreciation are to be based upon anything but original cost. To develop balance sheets at current market prices, it is also necessary to know the extent to which the changes in the balance sheet from year to year are the result of revaluation rather than changes in the total quantity of assets available.

Special tables are needed to show the implicit price deflators for final expenditures and for output originating in different industries as well as revaluations for national wealth and balance sheets, since such information is as much a part of economic behavior as are the real changes that take place in the economy.

Supplementary Breakdowns

In analyzing economic change, industrial breakdowns are especially important. Although this kind of information is shown in the input-output tables, most countries do not prepare these tables annually, and for many purposes quarterly or even monthly data by industry may be highly desirable. Current and constant price data by industry for short-run periods provide the basis for many economic indicators. In addition to total value added, breakdowns of wages and profits by industry are also very useful. For certain industrial sectors, e.g., the farm sector and the automobile sector, it may be desirable to present complete production accounts.

There is also a need for more detailed breakdowns of certain components of final expenditures on gross national product. Expenditures for consumption and for capital formation by households, enterprises, and government are particularly useful. Such breakdowns on a quarterly basis in both current and constant prices provide information on the flow of goods and services to final consumers and enable the analyst to see precisely what parts of final demand are expanding and contracting. For the government sector, it will be useful to show not only the actual expenditures on goods and services, but also total outlays by the different levels of government, in terms of major programs and types of transaction, e.g., transfer payments, subsidies, expenditures on goods and services, etc. For the foreign sector, special tabulations designed to highlight various critical elements in the balance of payments can be presented. In the household sector, breakdowns of income by size distribution and by social or demographic group will be useful. Finally, consideration should be given to regional breakdowns of all of these kinds of information. Thus, for example, time series showing the income of households within regions, the output of industries, and the expenditure of governments can be provided if the original data are developed to permit this. As already suggested, the volume of data involved in regional breakdowns may be so great that only a portion of it should be published, and the rest provided in machine readable form to those concerned with regional problems.

Social and Demographic Information

All of the data discussed thus far have been concerned with transactions. There are, however, related social and demographic data that also need to be considered. One of the most directly related sets of demographic data is employment by industry. It is important that the employment data be developed using precisely the same classifications used for income originating by industry. If this is done, it is then possible to derive income per worker by industry, and to show how this changes in different industries over time. Other demographic information is necessary to provide per capita measures of consumption or per capita regional data that can show differences in levels between different regions. Splitting the household sector into different economic groups has already been mentioned. In order to include social and demographic information more directly, sets of sample data are required that can be directly related to the economic accounts. Samples of households providing information on such things as wages, other income, financial transactions, and assets and liabilities need to be linked with social and demographic information relating to age, education, work status, family composition, place of residence, occupation, etc. Given a sufficiently large sample of such information, special tabulations of the economic characteristics of various groups in the economy would be possible. It will also be possible to use the sample data as the basis for testing various hypotheses or simulating various kinds of economic behavior.

Microdata sets, however, should not be confined to household data. Other forms of sample data can also be drawn from the operating records of government agencies. Thus, samples of tax returns from both households and businesses are possible. Social security records from establishments can do much to link the individual with the operation of producing units. For other sectors of the economy, many kinds of operating records exist that are valuable for economic research. It should be emphasized again that in the use of such records for economic analysis, provision must be made to preserve the confidentiality of the records.

Implementation of the Proposed System

This system has been designed to provide (1) a standardized set of integrated economic accounts, and (2) a system for interrelating these accounts with other economic and social information. The proposed system is, however, more than just a general framework into which different kinds of data can be fitted; it is built around specific economic constructs, and considers economic activity in terms of the interrelation between enterprises, government, and households. It is constructed so that the various aggregates and activities of the different sectors can be deconsolidated and decomposed into more detailed classification systems. In this connection, special emphasis is given to viewing the economy in terms of the operation of industrial and institutional sub-sectors. Emphasis has also been placed upon the development of microdata sets that can provide highly disaggregated information for use in developing special cross-tabulations or directly in simulation models. Although the proposed system has been developed largely in terms of the data system of the United States, the new revision of the UN system has also been considered.

Less Developed Countries

Less developed countries are usually severely limited in providing statistical information. Many may not be able to obtain the necessary data for major parts of the proposed national economic system and for other parts only broad estimates without the underlying detail may be possible. The proposed system is, however, constructed in such a manner that it can readily be adapted to such conditions. The basic structure of the system is of a telescoping nature, and in its most summary form there are relatively few major economic constructs and broad intersectoral relationships shown.

The limitation of statistical resources in these countries does not mean that estimates about the functioning of the economy are any less necessary. Estimates must be made from the best available evidence, and it is important that they be made in the context of a complete economic accounting system so that they will be internally consistent. First, the basic set of national income accounts in their most simplified form needs to be constructed. The final product side of the income and product account should show the use of resources for public and private consumption, and enterprise and government capital formation, together with the related information on imports and exports. In many countries, enterprise consumption and household capital formation may have to be ignored because of lack of statistical information. The income originating side of this account should show production originating in the market sector, production originating in households, and production originating in the government sector, together with information on indirect taxes and estimates of capital consumption.

The enterprise account should show the nature of the activity taking place in the market sector of the economy, and the relative importance of large producers as against the handicraft trades. For some countries where specific foreign companies are particularly important, it may be useful to show these foreign companies as a separate sector. On the outlay side of the account, the payments that enterprises make to the government and the income retained by enterprises are of particular importance. In the capital formation account for enterprises, the sources of financing obtained from the other sectors of the economy and from capital consumption and retained earnings will provide important information about the process of capital formation.

Government accounts are particularly important for these countries, and it is quite reasonable to expect government outlays to be shown in terms of expenditures for consumption, development, and durable goods. For this sector of the economy much more detailed information can be provided since data from government budgets and government internal accounts should be available even when other statistics are not.

For the household sector, much of the required information will have to be derived from the government and enterprise accounts. But specific information on the breakdown of the household sector into socioeconomic groups is extremely important. For example, it is necessary to know the number of people in the agricultural subsistence sector, compared with those in the urban service sector or the urban manufacturing sector. In a number of these countries special population surveys are undertaken, and it would be useful if these could be fitted into the other data relating to the household sector.

Finally, the external accounts also need to be shown in considerable detail, since the economic development of many less developed countries is closely related to the problems of international trade and payments.

Once the basic framework of national income accounting data is constructed, it is possible to generate additional related information. For example, constant price data can be provided for final expenditure if appropriate information on price changes for different commodities can be obtained. Some sort of industrial breakdown is generally possible, since in most cases the data for output are obtained on an industry basis. Deflation of the industry output data can also be carried out on the basis of price information which is usually obtainable. The degree of refinement in the statistical estimates will depend upon the kind of information available.

For some less developed countries it may be possible to construct summary input-output tables and highly aggregated financial data. For both estimation and analytic usefulness, these sets of information must be directly integrated with the basic national income accounts so that they augment information rather than provide a set of data that is inconsistent and not directly comparable.

Although the specific classifications used to show the structure of a less developed country must be adapted to the availability of information and to the particular structure of the country involved, it is very important that the basic information fit into a standardized economic accounting system. Highly specialized and unique sets of information seriously limit the ability of any country to compare its performance with that of similar countries and, with change over time, comparisons between time periods also become difficult. Therefore, these countries should use the same type of economic accounting system as developed countries, so that comparability over time and space can be maintained.

Developed Countries

For the developed countries, the proposed system serves two functions. First, it provides a framework for existing data, which insures consistency among the different kinds of information, and provides a logical place for each. Second, because it is comprehensive, the proposed system provides a checklist of important economic information and reveals statistical gaps that may exist for a particular country.

The proposed changes in the definitions of some major economic constructs and the sectoring of the economy would require more data than is provided by the present US system. For example, it will be necessary to estimate the capital formation of households and government in terms of development expenditures and durable goods, and through the perpetual inventory method and analysis of length of life to arrive at information on stocks of development outlays and durable goods for these sectors. From a technical standpoint, it is possible to develop these statistics on the basis of existing information. Some special studies might have to be made of the length of life of different durables, and decisions on amortization of development outlays would be required. For enterprise activities, studies would be needed of enterprise consumption and enterprise expenditures on research and development and education and training. To obtain estimates of imputed interest at the establishment level, plant and equipment data would be required for establishments in various industries, and to obtain imputed interest for enterprises, the value of net assets owned by various kinds of enterprises would also be required. Estimates of depreciation would have to be reworked to adjust them for length of life and replacement cost valuation.

Input-output and flow-of-funds data now exist on a basis that matches the national income accounts, but additional work needs to be done on extending the comparability to the more detailed subsector levels for both industries and institutions. The extension of the flow-of-funds data to sets of national balance sheets and the development of national wealth information require substantial additional information, as indicated by the Wealth Inventory Planning Study [33]. The recommendations in this study fit in with the type of information required for the proposed system.

Although the proposed national economic accounting system has been developed primarily in relation to western national accounts, the general structure is also relevant for countries using the material product concept of economic accounting. The material product concept views certain types of expenditures as intermediate rather than final goods, so that to obtain material product these must be eliminated from final expenditures, on the one hand, and from output, on the other. In countries where the government provides substantial amounts of services free, it is useful to show the interrelation between the enterprise sectors and the community sector. The proposed system provides this distinction—separating the activity of enterprises that sell their goods on the market from those that provide consumption goods free. Countries interested in using material product concepts are also interested in the full set of economic transactions taking place in their economic systems, and since the proposed set of national economic accounts is constructed in terms of these transactions it will be as directly relevant to the operation of these systems as to Western systems. Since market values in the material product countries do not have the same significance as they have in other countries, social and demographic information may assume a greater importance. Thus, for example, it may be important to observe directly the characteristics and behavior of household units and their changes over time.

The proposed national economic accounting system is intended as a general economic accounting framework. It has been developed to provide for the systematic treatment of the ever-expanding information about the operation of the economic system. It involves specific statistical requirements for the more aggregated comprehensive core of information. On the other hand, its system of deconsolidation and disaggregation provides for the increasing wealth of information that is becoming available in the more developed countries and that is required for the analysis of modern economic and social problems.

Appendix A

AN ILLUSTRATION OF THE COMPLETE REVISED UNITED NATIONS SYSTEM

Appendix **B**

THE REVISED UNITED NATIONS SYSTEM OF NATIONAL ACCOUNTS:

Table Forms for Class I,
Class II, and Class III Accounts

TABLE B–1

The Revised UN System: Table Form for Class I Accounts—
Consolidated for the Nation

Account 1. Gross Domestic Product and Expenditure

1.3.1	Compensation of employees (3.3.1)	2.2.20	Government final consumption expenditure (3.2.20)
1.3.2	Operating surplus (3.3.2)	2.2.30	Private final consumption expenditure (3.2.30)
1.3.3	Consumption of fixed capital (5.3.3)	4.2.5	Increase in stocks (5.2.5)
1.3.4	Indirect taxes (3.3.4)	4.2.6	Gross fixed capital formation (5.2.6)
1.3.5	*Less* Subsidies (3.3.5)	1.2.10	Exports of goods and services (6.2.10)
		1.1.10	*Less* Imports of goods and services ($-6.1.10$)
Gross domestic product		Expenditure on the gross domestic product	

Account 3. National Disposable Income and Its Appropriation

3.2.20	Government final consumption expenditure (2.2.20)	3.3.1	Compensation of employees (1.3.1)
3.2.30	Private final consumption expenditure (2.2.30)	3.4.2	Compensation of employees from the rest of the world, net ($6.4.1 - 6.3.1$)
3.7.1	Saving (5.7.1)	3.3.2	Operating surplus (1.3.2)
		3.4.10	Property and entrepreneurial income from the rest of the world, net ($6.4.9 - 6.4.8$)
		3.3.4	Indirect taxes (1.3.4)
		3.3.5	*Less* Subsidies (1.3.5)
		3.6.23	Other current transfers from the rest of the world, net ($6.6.22 - 6.6.21$)
Appropriation of disposable income		Disposable income	

(continued)

TABLE B–1 (concluded)

Account 5. Capital Finance

5.2.5	Increase in stocks (4.2.5)	5.7.1	Saving (3.7.1)
5.2.6	Gross fixed capital formation (4.2.6)	5.3.3	Consumption of fixed capital (1.3.3)
5.7.5	Purchases of intangible assets, n.e.c., from the rest of the world, net (6.7.5)	5.7.6	Capital transfers from the rest of the world, net (6.7.6)
5.7.8	Net lending to the rest of the world (5.7.9)		
Gross accumulation		**Finance of gross accumulation**	
5.8.0	Net acquisition of financial assets (6.8.0 + 5.9.0 − 6.9.0)	5.7.9	Net lending to the rest of the world (5.7.8)
		5.9.0	Net incurrence of liabilities (6.9.0 + 5.8.0 − 6.8.0)
Net acquisition of financial assets		**Net incurrence of liabilities plus net lending to the rest of the world**	

Account 6. All Accounts—External Transactions

Current Transactions

6.2.10	Exports of goods and services (1.2.10)	6.1.10	Imports of goods and services (− 1.1.10)
6.4.1	Compensation of employees from the rest of the world (3.4.2 + 6.3.1)	6.3.1	Compensation of employees to the rest of the world (3.3.1*)
6.4.9	Property and entrepreneurial income from the rest of the world (3.4.10 + 6.4.8)	6.4.8	Property and entrepreneurial income to the rest of the world (6.4.9 − 3.4.10)
6.6.22	Other current transfers from the rest of the world (3.6.23 + 6.6.21)	6.6.21	Other current transfers to the rest of the world (6.6.22 − 3.6.23)
		6.7.3	Surplus of the nation on current transactions (6.7.2)
Current receipts		**Disposal of current receipts**	

Capital Transactions

6.7.2	Surplus of the nation on current transactions (6.7.3)	6.7.5	Purchases of intangible assets n.e.c., from the rest of the world, net (5.7.5)
6.7.6	Capital transfers from the rest of the world, net (5.7.6)	6.8.0	Net acquisition of foreign financial assets (5.8.0 − 5.9.0 + 6.9.0)
6.9.0	Net incurrence of foreign liabilities (5.9.0 − 5.8.0 + 6.8.0)		
Receipts		**Disbursements**	

NOTE: Numbers in parentheses indicate accounts and item of counter-entry. An asterisk denotes "part of" item listed. Numbering system is that of the revised UN accounts.

TABLE B–2

The Revised UN System: Table Form for Class II Accounts—Production,
Consumption Expenditure, and Capital Formation

A. Commodities—Accounts 1, 2, and 4

Illustrative Account—b. Characteristic Products of Mining and Quarrying,
Manufacturing, and Electricity, Gas, and Water

1.1.1.1	Industrial commodities from domestic industrial activity (Cb 1.1.1.1)	1.2.1	Intermediate consumption, industries (CΣn 1.2.1*)
1.1.1.2	Industrial commodities from other domestic industries	1.2.2	Intermediate consumption, producers of government services (D 1.2.2*)
1.1.2	Industrial commodities from producers of government services (D 1.1.2*)	1.2.3	Intermediate consumption, producers of private nonprofit services to households (E 1.2.3*)
1.1.3	Industrial commodities from producers of private nonprofit services to households (E 1.1.3*)	2.2.4	Final consumption expenditure in the domestic market, households (Bd 2.2.4*)
1.1.11	Imports of industrial commodities, c.i.f.	4.2.5	Increase in stocks
1.3.4.1	Import duties, industrial commodities	4.2.6	Gross fixed capital formation
		1.2.11	Exports
Supply		Use	

B. Other Goods and Services—Accounts 1, 2, and 4

a. Sales of Other Goods and Services and Direct Imports of Government Services

1.1.4	Noncommodity sales, producers of government services (D 1.1.4)	1.2.2	Intermediate consumption, producers of government services (D 1.2.2*)
1.1.6	Noncommodity sales, producers of private nonprofit services to households (E 1.1.6)	2.2.4	Final consumption expenditure in the domestic market, households (Bd 2.2.4*)
1.1.8	Domestic services of households (F 1.1.8)		
1.1.12.2	Direct purchases abroad on current account, producers of government services		
Supply		Use	

b. Final Consumption Expenditure of Government Services

1.1.5	Services produced for own use (D 1.1.5)	2.2.20	Final consumption expenditure
Supply		Use	

(continued)

TABLE B–2 (continued)

c. Final Consumption Expenditure of Private Nonprofit Services to Households

1.1.7	Services produced for own use (E 1.1.7)	2.2.31	Final consumption expenditure
Supply		Use	

d. Final Consumption Expenditure of Households

2.2.4	Final consumption expenditure in the domestic market, households ($A\Sigma n$ 2.2.4 + Ba 2.2.4)	2.2.32	Final consumption expenditure, resident households
2.1.12.1	Direct purchases abroad, resident households	2.2.12.1	Direct purchases in the domestic market, nonresident households
Supply		Use	

C. Industries—Account 1, Production Account

Illustrative Account—b. Mining and Quarrying, Manufacturing, and Electricity, Gas, and Water

1.2.1	Intermediate consumption ($A\Sigma n$ 1.2.1)	1.1.1.1	Characteristic products of industrial activity (Ab 1.1.1.1)
1.3.1	Compensation of employees	1.1.1.3	Other products
1.3.2	Operating surplus		
1.3.3	Consumption of fixed capital		
1.3.4	Indirect taxes		
1.3.5	*Less* Subsidies		
Gross input		Gross output	

D. Producers of Government Services—Account 1, Production Account

1.2.2	Intermediate consumption ($A\Sigma n$ 1.2.2 + Ba 1.2.2)	1.1.5	Services produced for own use (Bb 1.1.5)
1.3.1	Compensation of employees	1.1.4	Noncommodity sales (Ba 1.1.4)
1.3.3	Consumption of fixed capital	1.1.2	Commodities produced ($A\Sigma n$ 1.1.2)
1.3.4	Indirect taxes		
Gross input		Gross output	

(continued)

TABLE B–2 (concluded)

E. Producers of Private Nonprofit Services to Households—Account 1,
Production Account

1.2.3	Intermediate consumption (AΣn 1.2.3)	1.1.7	Services produced for own use (Bc 1.1.7)
1.3.1	Compensation of employees	1.1.6	Noncommodity sales (Ba 1.1.6)
1.3.3	Consumption of fixed capital	1.1.3	Commodities produced (AΣn 1.1.3)
1.3.4	Indirect taxes		
Gross input		**Gross output**	

F. Domestic Services of Households

1.3.1	Compensation of employees	1.1.8	Domestic services (Ba 1.1.8)
Gross input		**Gross output**	

NOTE: See note to Table B–1.

TABLE B–3

The Revised UN System: Table Form for Class III Accounts—Income and Outlay and Capital Finance

A. Nonfinancial Enterprises, Corporate and Quasi-Corporate

Account 3. Income and Outlay Account

3.4.4	Withdrawals from entrepreneurial income of quasi-corporate enterprises	3.3.2	Operating surplus
3.4.6	Property income	3.4.5	Withdrawals from entrepreneurial income of quasi-corporate enterprises
	1. Interest		
	2. Dividends	3.4.7	Property income
	3. Rent		1. Interest
3.5.1	Net casualty insurance premiums		2. Dividends
			3. Rent
3.6.1	Direct taxes	3.5.2	Casualty insurance claims
	1. On income	3.6.7	Unfunded employee welfare contributions imputed
	2. Not elsewhere classified		
3.6.2	Fines and penalties		
3.6.8	Unfunded employee welfare benefits		
3.6.13	Current transfers, n.e.c., net		
3.7.1	Saving (A 5.7.1)		
Disbursements		**Receipts**	

Account 5. Capital Finance Account

5.2.5	Increase in stocks	5.7.1	Saving (A 3.7.1)
5.2.6	Gross fixed capital formation	5.3.3	Consumption of fixed capital
5.7.4	Purchases of land, net	5.7.6	Capital transfers, net
5.7.5	Purchases of intangible assets, n.e.c., net		
5.7.8	Net lending (A 5.7.9)		
Gross accumulation		**Finance of gross accumulation**	
5.8.1	Gold	5.7.9	Net lending (A 5.7.8)
5.8.2	Current and transferable deposits	5.9.4	Bills and bonds, short-term
		5.9.5	Bonds, long-term
5.8.3	Other deposits	5.9.6	Corporate equity securities, including capital participations
5.8.4	Bills and bonds, short-term		
5.8.5	Bonds, long-term	5.9.7	Short-term loans, n.e.c.

(continued)

TABLE B–3 (continued)

5.8.6	Corporate equity securities, including capital participations		5.9.8	Long-term loans, n.e.c.
5.8.7 and 8	Loans, n.e.c.		5.9.10	Proprietors' net additions to the accumulation of quasi-corporate enterprises
5.8.10	Proprietors' net additions to the accumulation of quasi-corporate enterprises		5.9.11	Trade credit and advances
5.8.11	Trade credit and advances		5.9.12 and 13	Other liabilities
5.8.12 and 13	Other financial assets			
Net acquisition of financial assets			Net incurrence of liabilities plus net lending	

B. Financial Institutions

Account 3. Income and Outlay Account

3.4.4	Withdrawals from entrepreneurial income of quasi-corporate enterprises		3.3.2	Operating surplus
3.4.6	Property income 1. Interest 2. Dividends 3. Rent		3.4.5	Withdrawals from entrepreneurial income of quasi-corporate enterprises
3.5.1	Net casualty insurance premiums		3.4.7	Property income 1. Interest 2. Dividends 3. Rent
3.5.4	Casualty insurance claims		3.5.2	Casualty insurance claims
3.6.1	Direct taxes 1. On income 2. Not elsewhere classified		3.5.3	Net casualty insurance premiums
3.6.2	Fines and penalties		3.6.7	Unfunded employee welfare contributions imputed
3.6.8	Unfunded employee welfare benefits			
3.6.13	Current transfers, n.e.c., net			
3.7.1	Saving (B 5.7.1)			
Disbursements			Receipts	

(continued)

TABLE B–3 (continued)

Account 5. Capital Finance Account

5.2.5	Increase in stocks		5.7.1	Saving (B 3.7.1)
5.2.6	Gross fixed capital formation		5.3.3	Consumption of fixed capital
5.7.4	Purchases of land, net		5.7.6	Capital transfers, net
5.7.5	Purchases of intangible assets, n.e.c., net			
5.7.8	Net lending (B 5.7.9)			

Gross accumulation

Finance of gross accumulation

5.8.1	Gold		5.7.9	Net lending (B 5.7.8)
5.8.2	Currency and transferable deposits		5.9.2	Currency issued by the central bank and transferable deposits
	Of which by monetary institutions, liability of:		5.9.3	Other deposits
			5.9.4	Bills and bonds, short-term
	i. Resident institutions		5.9.5	Bonds, long-term
	ii. Rest of the world		5.9.6	Corporate equity securities, including capital participations
5.8.3	Other deposits			
5.8.4	Bills and bonds, short-term		5.9.7	Short-term loans, n.e.c.
5.8.5	Bonds, long-term			Of which by monetary institutions to:
5.8.6	Corporate equity securities, including capital participations			i. Resident institutions
5.8.7	Short-term loans, n.e.c.			ii. Rest of the world
	i. Of which by the central bank, liability of the rest of the world		5.9.8	Long-term loans, n.e.c.
			5.9.9	Net equity of households on life insurance reserves and on pension funds
5.8.8	Long-term loans, n.e.c.			
5.8.10	Proprietors' net additions to the accumulation of quasi-corporate enterprises		5.9.10	Proprietors' net additions to the accumulation of quasi-corporate enterprises
5.8.11, 12, and 13	Other financial assets		5.9.11, 12, and 13	Other liabilities

Net acquisition of financial assets

Net incurrence of liabilities plus net lending

(continued)

TABLE B–3 (continued)

C. General Government

Account 3. Income and Outlay Account

3.2.20	Final consumption expenditure		3.3.2	Operating surplus
3.4.6	Property income 1. Interest on public debt 3. Rent		3.4.5	Withdrawals from entrepreneurial income of quasi-corporate government enterprises
3.5.1	Net casualty insurance premiums		3.4.7	Property income 1. Interest
3.3.5	Subsidies			2. Dividends
3.6.4	Social security benefits			3. Rent
3.6.5	Social assistance grants		3.5.2	Casualty insurance claims
3.6.6	Current transfers to private non-profit institutions serving households		3.3.4	Indirect taxes 1. Import duties 2. Other indirect taxes
3.6.8	Unfunded employee welfare benefits		3.6.1	Direct taxes 1. On income 2. Not elsewhere classified
3.6.9	Current transfers, n.e.c., to: 1. Residents 2. The rest of the world		3.6.2	Compulsory fees, fines, and penalties
3.7.1	Saving (C 5.7.1)		3.6.3	Social security contributions
			3.6.7	Unfunded employee welfare contributions imputed
			3.6.10	Current transfers, n.e.c., from: 1. Residents 2. The rest of the world
Disbursements			Receipts	

Account 5. Capital Finance Account

5.2.5	Increase in stocks		5.7.1	Saving (C 3.7.1)
5.2.6	Gross fixed capital formation		5.3.3	Consumption of fixed capital
5.7.4	Purchases of land, net		5.7.6	Capital transfers, net, from: i. Residents ii. The rest of the world
5.7.5	Purchases of intangible assets, n.e.c., net			
5.7.8	Net lending (C 5.7.9)			
Gross accumulation			Finance of gross accumulation	
5.8.1	Gold		5.7.9	Net lending (C 5.7.8)
5.8.2	Currency and transferable deposits Of which by central government, liability of: i. Resident institutions ii. Rest of the world		5.9.2	Currency issued by the treasury and transferable deposits
			5.9.3	Other deposits
			5.9.4	Bills and bonds, short-term
			5.9.5	Bonds, long-term
			5.9.7	Short-term loans, n.e.c.

(continued)

TABLE B–3 (continued)

5.8.3	Other deposits		5.9.8	Long-term loans, n.e.c.
5.8.4	Bills and bonds, short-term		5.9.11,	
5.8.5	Bonds, long-term		12, and	
5.8.6	Corporate equity securities, including capital participations		13	Other liabilities
5.8.7	Short-term loans, n.e.c.			
5.8.8	Long-term loans, n.e.c.			
5.8.10	Proprietors' net additions to the accumulation of quasi-corporate government enterprises			
5.8.11, 12, and				
13	Other financial assets			
Net acquisition of financial assets			Net incurrence of liabilities plus net lending	

D. Private Nonprofit Institutions Serving Households

Account 3. Income and Outlay Account

3.2.31	Final consumption expenditure		3.3.2	Operating surplus
3.4.6	Property income		3.4.7	Property income
	1. Interest			1. Interest
	3. Rent			2. Dividends
3.5.1	Net casualty insurance premiums			3. Rent
			3.5.2	Casualty insurance claims
3.6.1	Direct taxes		3.6.6	Current transfers to private nonprofit institutions
	1. On income			
	2. Not elsewhere classified		3.6.7	Unfunded employee welfare contributions imputed
3.6.2	Fines and penalties			
3.6.5	Social assistance grants			
3.6.8	Unfunded employee welfare benefits			
3.7.1	Saving (D 5.7.1)			
Disbursements			Receipts	

(continued)

TABLE B-3 (continued)

Account 5. Capital Finance Account

5.2.6	Gross fixed capital formation		5.7.1	Saving (D 3.7.1)
5.7.4	Purchases of land, net		5.3.3	Consumption of fixed capital
5.7.5	Purchases of intangible assets, n.e.c., net		5.7.6	Capital transfers, net
5.7.8	Net lending (D 5.7.9)			
Gross accumulation			**Finance of gross accumulation**	
5.8.1	Gold		5.7.9	Net lending (D 5.7.8)
5.8.2	Currency and transferable deposits		5.9.7 and 8	Loans, n.e.c.
5.8.3	Other deposits		5.9.11, 12, and 13	Other liabilities
5.8.4	Bills and bonds, short-term			
5.8.5	Bonds, long-term			
5.8.6	Corporate equity securities, including capital participations			
5.8.7, 8, 11, 12, and 13	Other financial assets			
Net acquisition of financial assets			**Net incurrence of liabilities plus net lending**	

E. Households, Including Private Unincorporated Nonfinancial Enterprises

Account 3. Income and Outlay Account

3.2.32	Final consumption expenditure		3.4.1	Compensation of employees
3.4.6	Property income		3.3.2	Operating surplus
	1 i. Consumer debt interest		3.4.5	Withdrawals from entrepreneurial income of quasi-corporate enterprises
	1 ii. Other interest			
	3. Rent			
3.5.1	Net casualty insurance premiums		3.4.7	Property income
				1. Interest
3.6.1	Direct taxes			2. Dividends
	1. On income			3. Rent
	2. Not elsewhere classified		3.5.2	Casualty insurance claims
3.6.2	Compulsory fees, fines, and penalties		3.6.4	Social security benefits
			3.6.5	Social assistance grants
3.6.3	Social security contributions		3.6.8	Unfunded employee welfare benefits
3.6.6	Current transfers to private non-profit institutions		3.6.12	Current transfers, n.e.c., from:

(continued)

TABLE B–3 (concluded)

3.6.7	Unfunded employee welfare contributions imputed	1. Residents	

3.6.11	Current transfers, n.e.c., to:
	    1. Residents
	    2. The rest of the world
		2. The rest of the world	

3.7.1	Saving (E 5.7.1)		

Disbursements   Receipts

Account 5. Capital Finance Account

5.2.5	Increase in stocks	5.7.1	Saving (E 3.7.1)
5.2.6	Gross fixed capital formation	5.3.3	Consumption of fixed capital
5.7.4	Purchases of land, net	5.7.6	Capital transfers, net
5.7.5	Purchases of intangible assets, n.e.c., net		
5.7.8	Net lending (E 5.7.9)		

Gross accumulation   Finance of gross accumulation

5.8.1	Gold	5.7.9	Net lending (E 5.7.8)
5.8.2	Currency and transferable deposits	5.9.7	Short-term loans, n.e.c.
5.8.3	Other deposits	5.9.8	Long-term loans, n.e.c.
5.8.4	Bills and bonds, short-term	5.9.11	Trade credit and advances
5.8.5	Bonds, long-term	5.9.12	
5.8.6	Corporate equity securities, including capital participations	and 13 Other liabilities	
5.8.7 and 8	Loans, n.e.c.		
5.8.9	Net equity of households on life insurance reserves and on pension funds		
5.8.10	Proprietors' net additions to the accumulation of quasi-corporate private enterprises		
5.8.11	Trade credit and advances		
5.8.12 and 13	Other financial assets		

Net acquisition of financial assets   Net incurrence of liabilities plus net lending

NOTE: See note to Table B–1.

Appendix C

THE PROPOSED
NATIONAL
ECONOMIC ACCOUNTS
FOR THE
UNITED STATES, 1966

TABLE C–1

The Proposed System: National Income and Product Account for the US, 1966

(billions of dollars)

INCOME ORIGINATING		FINAL EXPENDITURES	
1.1 Enterprise Sector	529.0	1.13 Consumption	590.0
a. Employee compensation	359.1	a. Households	435.7
b. Self-employed compensation	40.0	1. Market	339.4
		2. Nonmarket	96.3
c. Imputed interest on plant and equipment	50.0	b. Government	125.1
d. Net operating surplus	79.9	1. Market	73.1
		2. Nonmarket	52.0
		c. Enterprises	29.2
1.2 Government Sector	92.6		
a. Employee compensation	76.6	1.14 Gross Capital Formation	308.2
b. Imputed income from development and durables	16.0	a. Households	100.2
		1. Development	12.7
		2. Housing	17.2
1.3 Household Sector	38.4	3. Other durables	70.3
a. Nonmarket production	.9	b. Government	81.2
b. Imputed income from development and durables	37.5	1. Development	40.0
		2. Structures	24.2
		3. Other durables	17.0
1.4 National Income	660.0	c. Enterprises	126.8
		1. Development	26.0
1.5 Capital Consumption	165.5	2. Structures	35.1
a. Depreciation	122.5	3. Other durables	52.3
1. Enterprises	55.6	4. Change in inventories	13.4
2. Government	16.0		
3. Households	50.9	1.15 Exports	37.3
b. Amortization	43.0		
1. Enterprises	16.0	1.16 *Minus:* Imports	36.4
2. Government	20.0		
3. Households	7.0	1.17 Gross Domestic Product at Market Prices	899.1
1.6 Gross National Product at Factor Cost	825.5	1.18 Factor Income From Abroad	5.7
1.7 Business Transfers	2.7	1.19 *Minus:* Factor Income Sent Abroad	1.5
1.8 Business Consumption	18.0		
1.9 Indirect Taxes	65.1		
1.10 *Minus:* Subsidies	5.4		
1.11 Statistical Discrepancy	−2.6		
1.12 GROSS NATIONAL PRODUCT AT MARKET PRICES	903.3	1.20 GROSS NATIONAL PRODUCT AT MARKET PRICES	903.3

TABLE C–2a

The Proposed System: Enterprise Income and Outlay Account for the US, 1966

(billions of dollars)

2.1 Enterprise Consumption	29.2	2.6 Enterprise Income	529.0

2.1 Enterprise Consumption	29.2	2.6 Enterprise Income	529.0
a. Business consumption	18.7	a. Corporate	360.4
1. Mass media support	13.0	1. Employee compensation	275.9
2. Provision of consumption goods	5.7	2. Net interest paid	−2.4
b. Nonprofit consumption	10.5	3. Imputed interest on corporate net assets	40.0
1. Religious	5.0	4. Corporate net profits	46.8
2. Health, education, welfare	3.5	b. Noncorporate	139.2
3. Other	2.0	1. Employee compensation	59.2
2.2 Payments to Households	489.3	2. Net interest paid	11.2
a. Employee compensation	359.1	3. Self-employed compensation	40.0
b. Interest paid	40.9	4. Imputed interest on noncorporate net assets	15.0
c. Dividends	20.5	5. Noncorporate net profits	13.8
Plus: (d + e)		c. Government enterprises	11.3
d. Proprietor and rental income	79.1	1. Employee compensation	8.0
e. Adjustments	−10.3	2. Surplus	3.3
Or *plus:* (f + g + h)		d. Nonprofit institutions	14.0
f. Self-employed compensation	40.0	1. Employee compensation	16.0
g. Imputed interest on noncorporate assets	15.0	2. Net interest paid	−2.0
h. Net noncorporate profits	13.8	e. Rest of the world	4.2
2.3 Direct Taxes and Other Payments	41.8	1. Corporate profits	3.3
a. Corporate profits tax	34.5	2. Net interest	.9
b. Government enterprise surplus	3.3	2.7 Transfers to Nonprofit Institutions From Households	6.5
c. Interest paid to government	4.0	2.8 Enterprise Receipts Expensed	20.7
2.4 Retained Enterprise Income	35.2	a. Business consumption	18.0
a. Undistributed corporate profits	27.7	b. Business transfers to nonprofit institutions and consumer bad debts	2.7
b. Corporate profits adjustments	6.4	2.9 Interest Paid by Consumers	25.3
c. Retained nonprofit income	1.0	3.0 Interest Paid by Government	13.9
2.5 PAYMENTS AND RETAINED INCOME OF ENTERPRISES	595.4	3.1 RECEIPTS OF ENTERPRISES	595.4

TABLE C–2b

The Proposed System: Enterprise Capital Formation Account for the US, 1966

(billions of dollars)

2.10 Development Expenditures	26.0	2.15 Enterprise Capital Consumption	71.6
a. Research and development	18.0	a. Depreciation	55.6
b. Education and training	8.0	1. Corporate	39.0
		2. Noncorporate	15.6
		3. Nonprofit institutions	1.0
2.11 Durables Expenditures	87.4	b. Amortization	16.0
a. Structures	35.1	1. Corporate	12.0
b. Other durables	52.3	2. Noncorporate	4.0
2.12 Change in Inventories	13.4	2.16 Retained Income	35.1
		a. Corporate	34.1
2.13 Net Foreign Investment	2.2	b. Nonprofit	1.0
		2.17 Net Borrowing From (+) or Lending to (−) Other Sectors	+24.9
		a. Households	+17.7
		b. Government	+ 7.2
		2.18 Statistical Discrepancy	−2.6
2.14 GROSS ENTERPRISE CAPITAL FORMATION	129.0	2.19 GROSS SAVING AND NET BORROWING OR LENDING BY ENTERPRISES	129.0

TABLE C–3a

The Proposed System: Government Income and Outlay Account for the US, 1966

(billions of dollars)

3.1	Consumption	125.1	3.7	Indirect Taxes	65.1
	a. Current expenditures	73.1		a. Sales	17.7
	b. Imputed services of de-			b. Excise	13.2
	velopment and durables	52.0		c. Property	24.3
	1. Imputed interest	16.0		d. Other	9.9
	2. Capital consumption	16.0			
	3. Amortization	20.0	3.8	Direct Taxes and Other	
				Payments by Enterprises	41.8
3.2	Subsidies	5.4		a. Corporate profits tax	34.5
				b. Surplus of government	
3.3	Transfers to Households	41.2		enterprises	3.3
	a. Social insurance	29.1		c. Interest	4.0
	b. Other insurance and pen-				
	sions	5.6	3.9	Tax Payments by	
	c. Public assistance	4.3		Households	113.4
	d. Other	2.2		a. Social insurance contri-	
				butions	38.2
3.4	Transfers to Abroad	2.3		b. Income taxes	75.2
3.5	Current Surplus	48.4	3.10	Transfers From Abroad	*
			3.11	Imputed Income From	
				Development and	
				Durables	16.0
				a. Development	6.0
				b. Durables	10.0
			3.12	*Minus:* Interest Paid	13.9
3.6	GOVERNMENT				
	CURRENT OUTLAYS		3.13	GOVERNMENT	
	AND SURPLUS	222.4		RECEIPTS	222.4

NOTE: An asterisk denotes less than 0.05.

TABLE C–3b

The Proposed System: Government Capital Formation Account for the US, 1966

(billions of dollars)

3.13 Development Expenditures	40.0	3.17 Capital Consumption	36.0
a. Research and development	10.0	a. Depreciation	16.0
b. Education	20.0	b. Amortization	20.0
c. Health	10.0	3.18 Current Surplus	48.4
3.14 Structures Expenditures	24.2	3.19 Net Borrowing From (+) or Lending to (−) Other Sectors	−3.2
a. Buildings	8.9	a. Households	4.0
b. Highways and streets	8.3	b. Enterprises	−7.2
c. Other	7.0		
3.15 Other Durables Expenditures	17.0		____
3.16 GROSS GOVERNMENT CAPITAL FORMATION	81.2	3.20 GROSS SAVING AND NET BORROWING OR LENDING BY GOVERNMENT	81.2

TABLE C–4a

The Proposed System: Household Income and Outlay Account for the US, 1966

(billions of dollars)

4.1	Tax Payments	113.4	4.8	Payments by Enterprises	489.3
	a. Social security	38.2		a. Employee compensation	359.1
	b. Income taxes	75.2		b. Interest payments	40.9
				c. Dividends	20.5
4.2	DISPOSABLE INCOME	506.8		d. Self-employed compensation	40.0
				e. Imputed interest on proprietor net assets	15.0
4.3	Consumption	435.7		f. Proprietor net profits	13.8
	a. Current expenditures	339.4			
	b. Nonmarket production	.9	4.9	Compensation of Government Employees	76.6
	c. Services of development and durable goods	95.4			
	1. Imputed interest	37.5	4.10	Transfers From Government	41.2
	2. Capital consumption	50.9		a. Social insurance	29.1
	3. Amortization	7.0		b. Other insurance and pensions	5.6
				c. Public assistance	4.3
4.4	Transfers to Nonprofit Institutions	6.5		d. Other	2.2
4.5	Transfers to Abroad	.6	4.11	Transfers From Abroad	*
4.6	Current Saving	64.0	4.12	Income Originating in Households	38.4
				a. Nonmarket production	.9
				b. Net imputed income	37.5
				1. Owner-occupied housing	23.5
				2. Automobiles	5.0
				3. Other durables	7.0
				4. Development outlays	2.0
			4.13	*Minus:* Interest Paid	25.3
4.7	PERSONAL CURRENT OUTLAY AND SAVING	620.2	4.14	PERSONAL INCOME	620.2

NOTE: An asterisk denotes less than 0.05.

TABLE C–4b

The Proposed System: Household Capital Formation Account for the US, 1966

(billions of dollars)

4.14 Development Expenditures	12.7	4.17 Capital Consumption	57.9
a. Health	5.0	a. Depreciation	50.9
b. Education	6.7	1. Owner-occupied housing	7.9
c. Other	1.0	2. Automobiles	18.0
		3. Other	25.0
4.15 Durables Expenditures	87.5	b. Amortization	7.0
a. Owner-occupied housing	17.2	1. Health	3.5
b. Automobiles	29.9	2. Education	3.0
c. Other	40.4	3. Other	.5
		4.18 Current Saving	64.0
		4.19 Net Borrowing From (+) or Lending to (−) Other Sectors	−21.7
		a. Enterprises	−17.7
		b. Government	− 4.0
4.16 Gross Capital Formation by Households	100.2	4.20 Gross Saving and Net Borrowing or Lending by Households	100.2

TABLE C–5

The Proposed System: External Transactions Account for the US, 1966

(billions of dollars)

5.1 Exports	37.3	5.6 Imports	36.4
5.2 Factor income from abroad	5.7	5.7 Factor income to abroad	1.5
5.3 Transfers to households	*	5.8 Transfers from households	.6
5.4 Transfers to government	*	5.9 Transfers from government	2.3
		5.10 Net foreign investment	2.2
5.5 Receipts From Abroad	43.0	5.11 Payments to Abroad and Net Foreign Investment	43.0

NOTE: An asterisk denotes less than 0.05.

TABLE C–6

The Proposed System: Form for the Input-Output Current Account

	I. INTERMEDIATE SALES												II. FINAL SALES							III
	A. Enterprises									B. Government Industry	C. Household Industry	D. Rest of the World Industry	A. Households	B. Enterprises	C. Change in Inventories	D. Federal Government	E. State and Local Government	F. Exports	G. *Minus:* Imports	Value of Sales
		Agriculture				Mining		(Industries 6 to 82)												
		1. Livestock and livestock products	2. Other agricultural products	3. Forestry, fishery products	4. Agricultural, forestry, fishery services	5. Iron and ferroalloy ores mining	.	.	83. Scrap, used and secondhand goods											

I. PURCHASES BY:
  A. Enterprises
    Agriculture
    1. Livestock and livestock products
    2. Other agricultural products
    3. Forestry, fishery products
    4. Agricultural services
    Mining
    5. Iron and ferroalloy ores

    . (Industries 6 to 82)

    83. Scrap and secondhand goods
  B. Government Industry
  C. Household Industry
  D. Rest of World Industry
II. GROSS PRODUCT AT FACTOR COST
  A. Compensation of Employees
  B. Compensation of Self-Employed
  C. Imputed Interest on Capital
  D. Net Operating Surplus
  E. Capital Consumption
III. VALUE OF PRODUCT

TABLE C–7

The Proposed System: Form for the Input-Output Capital Account

	A. Enterprises	Agriculture	1. Livestock and products	2. Other agricultural products	3. Forestry, fishery products	4. Agricultural services	Mining	6. Iron and ferroalloy ores	.	. (Industries 6 to 82)	83. Scrap and secondhand goods	B. Government Industry	C. Household Industry	D. Rest of World Industry	Total Domestic Production Sectors

I. GROSS DOMESTIC
   INVESTMENT
   A. Enterprises
      Development expenditures
      1. Research and development
      2. Education and training
      Structures
      3. Residential rental buildings
      4. Commercial buildings
      5. Industrial buildings
      6. Institutional buildings
      7. Other construction
      Producer durables
      8. Furniture and fixtures
      9. Fabricated metal products
      .
      . (Producer durables 10 to 30)
      .
      Change in inventories
      31. Raw materials
      32. Work in process
      33. Finished goods
   B. Government
      34. Development expenditures
      35. Buildings
      36. Highways
      37. Other
   C. Households
      38. Development expenditures
      39. Owner-occupied housing
      40. Automobiles
      41. Other consumer durables
II. SOURCES OF GROSS
    SAVING
    A. Capital Consumption
    B. Amortization
    C. Net Operating Surplus
       or Saving
    D. Net Financial Balance

TABLE C–8

The Proposed System: Form for the International Trade Account

Areas and Countries

I. EXPORTS
   A. Enterprises
      Agriculture
      1. Livestock and livestock products
      2. Other agricultural products
      3. Forestry and fishery products
      4. Agricultural services
      Mining
      5. Iron and ferroalloy ores

      . (Industries 6 to 82)

      83. Scrap and secondhand goods
   B. Government
   C. Households

II. IMPORTS
   A. Enterprises
      Agriculture
      1. Livestock and livestock products
      2. Other agricultural products
      3. Forestry and fishery products
      4. Agricultural services
      Mining
      5. Iron and ferroalloy ores

      . (Industries 6 to 82)

      83. Scrap and secondhand goods
   B. Government
   C. Households

III. NET TRADE BALANCE

TABLE C–9a

The Proposed System: Form for the Deconsolidated Enterprise Income and
Outlay Account

	A. Corporate Enterprise	1. Agriculture	2. Mining	3. Contract construction	. . .	10. Services	B. Noncorporate Enterprises (Industries 1–10)	C. Government Enterprises (Industries 1–10)	D. Nonprofit Institutions (Industries 1–10)	TOTAL, ALL ENTERPRISES

I. ENTERPRISE RECEIPTS
  A. Income Originating in Enterprises
    1. Labor cost
      a. Compensation of employees
      b. Compensation of self-employed
    2. Interest cost
      a. Net interest paid
      b. Imputed interest on capital
    3. Profits
      a. Book value
      b. Adjustments to profits
  B. Transfers From Households
  C. Imputed Income From Business Consumption and Transfers
  D. Income From Abroad
  E. Transfers From the Enterprise Sector

II. ENTERPRISE OUTLAYS AND RETAINED INCOME
  A. Enterprise Consumption
  B. Payments to Individuals
    1. Compensation of employees
    2. Interest paid
    3. Dividends
    4. Profits paid
  C. Tax Payments to Government
  D. Transfers to Enterprise Sectors
  E. Income Retained

TABLE C–9b

The Proposed System: Form for the Deconsolidated Government Income and
Outlay Account

	A. Federal Government	B. State Governments	1. Alabama	2. Alaska	. . .	50. Wyoming	C. Local Governments	(major cities and groupings of other local governments)	TOTAL, ALL GOVERNMENTS
I. GOVERNMENT RECEIPTS									
A. Indirect Taxes									
1. Sales taxes									
2. Excise taxes									
3. Property taxes									
4. Other									
B. Direct Taxes									
5. Corporate profits tax									
6. Social insurance contributions									
7. Personal income taxes									
C. Imputed Income From Durables and Past Development Outlays									
D. Transfers From Abroad									
E. Transfers From Government									
II. GOVERNMENT OUTLAYS AND CURRENT SURPLUS									
A. Government Consumption									
1. Current expenditures									
2. Services provided by stock of durables and past development outlays									
3. Capital consumption									
4. Amortization									
B. Subsidies									
C. Transfers to Households									
1. Social insurance									
2. Other insurance and pensions									
3. Public assistance									
4. Other									
D. Transfers to Abroad									
E. Transfers to Governments									
F. Current Surplus									

TABLE C–9c

The Proposed System: Form for the Deconsolidated Household Income and
Outlay Account

	A. Proprietors (Industries 1–10)	B. Employees (Industries 1–10)	C. Other	1. Retired population	2. Institutional population	3. Other	TOTAL, ALL HOUSEHOLDS

I. PERSONAL INCOME
  A. Income Payments
    1. Employee compensation
    2. Interest received
    3. Dividends
    4. Profits paid
  B. Transfers From Government
    1. Social insurance
    2. Other insurance and pensions
    3. Public assistance
    4. Other
  C. Transfers From Abroad
  D. Income Originating in Households
    1. Nonmarket production
    2. Imputed interest on household capital
  E. Transfers From Households

II. PERSONAL OUTLAY AND SAVING
  A. Tax Payments
  B. Consumption
    1. Current expenditures
    2. Net services of durables and past
       development outlays
    3. Capital consumption
    4. Amortization
  C. Transfers to Nonprofit Institutions
  D. Transfers to Abroad
  E. Transfers to Households
  F. Current Saving

TABLE C–10

The Proposed System: Form for the Asset and Liability Transactions Account

| | Subsector Classifications for | | | |
	Enterprises	Government	Household	TOTAL DOMESTIC

I. TOTAL ASSETS
   A. Development Expenditures
   B. Durables Expenditures
      1. Structures
      2. Producer durables
      3. Consumer durables
      4. Land
   C. Inventories
   D. Financial Assets
      1. Currency and demand deposits
      2. Other bank deposits and shares
      3. Life insurance reserves, private
      4. Pension funds, private
      5. Pension funds, government
      6. Consumer debt
      7. Trade debt
      8. Loans on securities
      9. Bank loans, n.e.c.
      10. Other loans
      11. Mortgages
      12. Bonds and notes
      13. Other financial assets

II. TOTAL LIABILITIES AND
    EQUITIES
   A. Liabilities
      1. Currency and demand deposits
      2. Other bank deposits and shares
      3. Life insurance reserves, private
      4. Pension funds, private
      5. Pension funds, government
      6. Consumer debt
      7. Trade debt
      8. Loans on securities
      9. Bank loans, n.e.c.
      10. Other loans
      11. Mortgages
      12. Bonds and notes
      13. Other liabilities
   B. Equities
      1. Retained income
      2. Realized capital gains

TABLE C–11

The Proposed System: Form for the Balance of Payments Account

Areas and Countries

I. NET TRADE BALANCE

II. NET PAYMENTS
1. Transfers, net
   a. Private
   b. Government
2. Private investment, net
   a. Direct
   b. Foreign securities sold in U.S.
   c. Redemptions
   d. Other transactions in foreign securities
   e. Other long-term, net
   f. Short-term, net
3. Government investment, net
   a. Long-term capital
   b. Scheduled loan repayments
   c. Nonscheduled loan repayments and selloffs
   d. Foreign currency holdings and short-term claims
4. Foreign capital, net

III. NET CHANGE IN MONETARY RESERVE ASSETS

TABLE C–12

The Proposed System: Form for the National Wealth Account

	A. Enterprises Agriculture	1. Livestock and products	2. Other agricultural products	3. Forestry, fishery products	4. Agricultural services Mining	5. Iron and ferroalloy ores	. . (Industries 6 to 82)	83. Scrap and secondhand goods B. Government Industry C. Household Industry	TOTAL, DOMESTIC PRODUCTION SECTORS
I. ASSETS									
A. Enterprises									
Development expenditures									
1. Research and development									
2. Education and training									
Structures									
3. Residential rental buildings									
4. Commercial buildings									
5. Industrial buildings									
6. Institutional buildings									
7. Other construction									
Producer durables									
8. Furniture and fixtures									
9. Fabricated metal products									
. (Producer durables 10 to 30)									
Change in inventories									
31. Raw materials									
32. Work in process									
33. Finished goods									
B. Government									
34. Development expenditures									
35. Buildings									
36. Highways									
37. Other									
C. Households									
38. Development expenditures									
39. Owner-occupied housing									
40. Automobiles									
41. Other consumer durables									
II. EQUITIES									
A. Net Operating Surplus									
B. Net Financial Balance									
C. Revaluation of Assets									

TABLE C–13

The Proposed System: Form for the National Balance Sheet

	Subsector Classifications for			
	Enterprises	Government	Household	TOTAL

I. TOTAL ASSETS
- A. Development Expenditures
- B. Durable Goods Expenditures
  - 1. Structures
  - 2. Producer durables
  - 3. Consumer durables
  - 4. Land
- C. Inventories
- D. Financial Assets
  - 1. Currency and demand deposits
  - 2. Other bank deposits and shares
  - 3. Life insurance reserves, private
  - 4. Pension funds, private
  - 5. Pension funds, government
  - 6. Consumer debt
  - 7. Trade debt
  - 8. Loans on securities
  - 9. Bank loans, n.e.c.
  - 10. Other loans
  - 11. Mortgages
  - 12. Bonds and notes
  - 13. Other financial assets

II. TOTAL LIABILITIES AND EQUITIES
- A. Liabilities
  - 1. Currency and demand deposits
  - 2. Other bank deposits and shares
  - 3. Life insurance reserves, private
  - 4. Pension funds, private
  - 5. Pension funds, government
  - 6. Consumer debt
  - 7. Trade debt
  - 8. Loans on securities
  - 9. Bank loans, n.e.c.
  - 10. Other loans
  - 11. Mortgages
  - 12. Bonds and notes
  - 13. Other liabilities
- B. Equities
  - 1. Retained income
  - 2. Realized capital gains
  - 3. Unrealized capital gains

BIBLIOGRAPHY

1. *U. S. Income and Output,* Supplement to *Survey of Current Business,* November 1958, U. S. Department of Commerce.
2. *A System of National Accounts and Supporting Tables,* United Nations, ST/STAT/SER.F/2, July 1953.
3. "Proposals for Revising the SNA, 1952," United Nations, E/CN.3/345, 28 June 1966.
4. Wesley C. Mitchell, Willford I. King, Frederick R. Macaulay, and Oswald W. Knauth, *Income in the United States: Its Amount and Distribution, 1909–1919,* New York, 1921.
5. Oswald W. Knauth, *Distribution of Income by States in 1919,* National Bureau of Economic Research, New York, 1922.
6. Maurice Leven, *Income in the Various States: Its Sources and Distribution, 1919, 1920, and 1921,* National Bureau of Economic Research, New York, 1925.
7. Willford I. King, *Employment, Hours and Earnings in Prosperity and Depression, United States, 1920–22,* National Bureau of Economic Research, New York, 1923.
8. ———, *The National Income and Its Purchasing Power,* National Bureau of Economic Research, New York, 1930.
9. Simon Kuznets, *National Income and Capital Formation, 1919–1935,* National Bureau of Economic Research, New York, 1937.
10. Milton Gilbert and George Jaszi, "National Product and Income Statistics," *Dun's Review,* February 1944; reprinted in *Readings in the Theory of Income Distribution,* published for the American Economic Association by Blakiston, 1946.
11. "National Income," Supplement to *Survey of Current Business,* July 1947, U. S. Department of Commerce.

12. "National Income," Supplement to *Survey of Current Business,* November 1954, U. S. Department of Commerce.
13. Wassily W. Leontief, *The Structure of the American Economy, 1919–1929,* Cambridge, Mass., 1941.
14. Jerome Cornfield, W. Duane Evans, and Marvin Hoffenberg, "Full Employment Patterns, 1950," *Monthly Labor Review,* Vol. 64, pp. 163–190 and 420–432, February and March 1947.
15. Morris A. Copeland, *A Study of Moneyflows in the United States,* National Bureau of Economic Research, New York, 1952.
16. Board of Governors of the Federal Reserve System, *Flow of Funds in the United States, 1939–1953,* Washington, 1955, and succeeding issues of the *Federal Reserve Bulletin.*
17. National Accounts Review Committee, "The National Economic Accounts of the United States," published in *Hearings before the Subcommittee on Economic Statistics of the Joint Economic Committee,* Washington, 1957; reissued as *The National Economic Accounts of the United States: Review, Appraisal, and Recommendations,* National Bureau of Economic Research, New York, 1958.
18. *The National Income and Product Accounts of the United States, 1929–1965,* Supplement to *Survey of Current Business,* August 1966, U. S. Department of Commerce.
19. Ragnar Frisch, *National Regnskapet* (National Accounting), Oslo, 1940.
20. Ed. Van Cleeff, "National Boekhouding, Proeve van een Jaaroverzicht Nederland, 1938," *De Economist,* Haarlem, 1941.
21. Richard Stone, *Measurement of National Income and the Construction of Social Accounts,* League of Nations Studies and Reports on Statistical Methods No. 7, 1947.
22. F. Thomas Juster, *Household Capital Formation and Financing, 1897–1962,* National Bureau of Economic Research, 1966.
23. John W. Kendrick, "Studies in the National Income Accounts," *47th Annual Report of the National Bureau of Economic Research,* June 1967, pp. 9–15; "The Expansion of Imputations in the National Income Accounts," paper presented at the meeting of the Southern Economic Association, Atlanta, Georgia, November 1966 (mimeographed), and "Restructuring the National Income Accounts for Investment and Growth Analysis," *Statistisk Tidskrift,* 1966:5.

24. Board of Governors of the Federal Reserve System, *Flow of Funds Accounts 1945–1967,* February 1968.
25. George J. Stigler, *Capital and Rates of Return in Manufacturing Industries,* Princeton University Press for the National Bureau of Economic Research, 1960.
26. James H. Schulz, "The Future Economic Circumstances of the Aged: A Simulation Projection, 1980," *Yale Economic Essays,* Vol. 7, No. 1, Spring 1967.
27. Joseph A. Pechman, "Simulation Study of Federal Individual Income Tax Returns," in *Annual Report of the Brookings Institution,* 1967, p. 58.
28. "Compustat Tapes," provided on a quarterly basis by Standard Statistics Co.
29. Helen Stone Tice, "Depreciation, Obsolescence, and the Measurement of the Aggregate Capital Stock of the United States, 1900–1962," Yale University Ph.D. dissertation; also in *Review of Income and Wealth,* Series 13, No. 2, June 1967, pp. 119–154.
30. George Jaszi, R. C. Wasson, and L. Grose, "Expansion of Fixed Business Capital in the United States: Rapid Postwar Growth—Rise Slackens," *Survey of Current Business,* November 1962, p. 10.
31. Raymond W. Goldsmith, *A Study of Saving in the United States,* Princeton, 1955–56.
32. John A. Gorman, "The Relationship of Balance Sheets and Wealth Estimates to National Income Accounts," in *Measuring the Nation's Wealth,* Studies in Income and Wealth 29, National Bureau of Economic Research, New York, 1964.
33. *Measuring the Nation's Wealth,* materials developed by the Wealth Inventory Planning Study, George Washington University, and presented by the Conference on Research in Income and Wealth to the Joint Economic Committee, Washington, D.C., December 1964; reissued by the National Bureau of Economic Research as Vol. 29 of *Studies in Income and Wealth.*

INDEX